Praise for *Ecospirituality*

"What happens when faith traditions engage the natural world prayer-
fully and imaginatively? This book is a marvelous means for expl⌐
rich resources within Christianity and other religious ⊦⌐
inspire love of the natural world: grounding faith i⌐ ˙

—Lisa E. Da⊦˙˙˙

Cali⸜

"In this fluently written and timely text, the a⸜   ⸜ positive
pedagogical atmosphere of inquiry through a⸜   ⸜est engagement
with traditional and contemporary texts on ecospirituality, while
also engaging the heart by fostering practice. She invites readers to
develop kinship with other creatures, providing inspiring exemplars,
while also encouraging proactive greening of spiritual practices. Her
bold synthesis weaves together insights from diverse religious traditions and ecofeminist theories. This book deserves to be widely used
and appreciated."

—Celia Deane-Drummond, senior research fellow in theology
and director of the *Laudato Si* Research Institute,
Campion Hall, University of Oxford

"Rachel Wheeler begins this timely and important book by inviting
us to exchange 'seeking' language for 'relating' or 'dwelling' language
as a way to describe the spiritual life: a helpful reframing that calls
us to discern the Sacred in the natural world rather than striving to
discover it outside of our embodied earthly experience. Drawing on
resources from Christian and other religious traditions, Wheeler's
insights help us recognize the myriad ways that our current ecological
and climate crisis is intertwined with racialized, gendered, and economic injustices, and she offers practical wisdom and practices that
can help us begin to heal."

—Timothy Robinson, Alberta H. and Harold L. Lunger Associate
Professor of Spiritual Disciplines and Resources,
Brite Divinity School at Texas Christian University

ecospirituality

eco spirit- uality

AN INTRODUCTION

RACHEL WHEELER

FORTRESS PRESS
MINNEAPOLIS

ECOSPIRITUALITY
An Introduction

Scripture quotations are from New Revised Standard Version Bible, copyright © 1989 National Council of the Churches of Christ in the United States of America. Used by permission. All rights reserved worldwide.

Cover design: Josh Dingle at LoveArts Design

Print ISBN: 978-1-5064-7386-4
eBook ISBN: 978-1-5064-7387-1

Whatever I know as a woman about spirituality I have learned from my body encountering Earth. Soul and soil are not separate. Neither are mind and spirit, nor water and tears.

—Terry Tempest Williams, *Erosion: Essays of Undoing*

Contents

Dedication and Gratitude

This book is dedicated to the students who have learned with me in eco-Bible and ecospirituality courses at the University of Portland. Their contemplative awareness, curiosity, creativity, and compassion inspire me. I especially appreciate those students who experienced forest therapy with me in Mount Tabor Park in Portland and Tyler Wagner and the students with whom I learned during an ecojustice immersion led by Meg Bender-Stephanski and Brittany D'Souza. When, during a reflection circle, a student recalled Robin Wall Kimmerer's grammar of animacy from our ecospirituality class, I almost melted with gratitude and joy! Many thanks to Meg, Madison Thibado, and Macey Schondel for allowing me to share words from their class assignments in chapter 6. I also dedicate this work to the students who faced challenges learning with me during the Covid-19 pandemic with special courage and took to heart our class ecospiritual practices in order to sustain that courage.

In my classes, we often begin with a short ritual of dedication, invoking family members or friends whom we love, famous people or ancestors who inspire us, favorite animal populations or sacred spaces we endeavor to protect and preserve. We do this in order to connect our learning with others who will benefit from our learning, directly and indirectly. We acknowledge together that we do not pursue knowledge just for its own sake or for what it may help us do to earn money or enhance our reputation; instead, we acknowledge a relationship between the energy we put into our learning and work together and the present and future flourishing of our communities, inclusive of human and other-than-human members. May your reading of this book and my writing of it promote actions and heart-dispositions that will contribute to the flourishing of the Earth community! I invite you to voice your own intention as you begin this book as well.

I express gratitude to my colleagues and peers at the University of Portland and in the Society for the Study of Christian Spirituality. The regular writing company of Shannon McAlister, Molly Hiro, Christi Hancock, Matthew Warshawsky, Kristin Sweeney, Alexa Dare, Brandy Daniels, Nina Henrichs-Tarasenkova, and David Turnbloom has numerous times sharpened my focus and inspired me—I thank each of you! Thanks also to Matthew Wickman, Mary Frohlich, Tim Robinson, and Lisa Dahill for conversational support on such intriguing topics as religious affects and engaging how forests think as collaborators in the Spirituality and Imagination research group formed with a grant from Brigham Young University's Humanities Center. I especially thank Lisa Dahill for sharing class syllabi with me as I began teaching; her exuberant presentation style is marvelously captured on the pages of these documents, and they helped me begin to shape my own early work teaching and writing.

I feel special gratitude for the patient persistence and insightful guidance of my editor at Fortress Press, Emily King. Her flexibility and firmness formed the perfect combination for my envisioning and completing the project of translating a course into a book. I learned so much working with her. Lastly, I thank my partner, Winston Wheeler, for his patient and caring company and love. May we continue to live within a world that together we love ever more passionately!

Introduction
What Is Ecospirituality?

Ecology and spirituality are fundamentally connected
because deep ecological awareness, ultimately, is spiritual
awareness.

—Fritjof Capra

Ecospirituality is a relatively new word indicating a particular form of
spirituality: *ecological* spirituality. There are a lot of words that people
use today to modify the word spirituality. For instance, people speak
of *contemplative* spirituality, *Franciscan* spirituality, *Buddhist* spirituality, and *feminist* spirituality. Each phrase expresses something significant about spirituality as a way of life informed by a particular
worldview or set of commitments. And yet what is spirituality itself?
Many people self-identify these days as "spiritual but not religious."
In fact, people do this so frequently that an acronym for this self-
identification has emerged: SBNR. Of course, people mean different
things when using this self-identifier, but often they mean to affirm
what they understand as an essential aspect of being human ("spiritual") in contrast to belonging to a recognized religious or philosophical tradition. For this book, a working definition of spirituality is
simply the way one relates to or with the sacred, or the way the sacred
informs one's way of being in the world. Because ecology has to do
with one's *home*—the root meaning of "eco"—ecological spirituality
or *ecospirituality* describes how one relates to the sacred within the
context of our natural, global, and even cosmic ecosystems (or homes)
of which we all form a part.

In contrast to this definition of ecospirituality, most definitions of spirituality emphasize *seeking* the sacred rather than *relating* to or with the sacred. For instance, *contemplative* spirituality describes a way of life that is lived out of a commitment to seeking to realize the sacred by means of a contemplative life orientation and contemplative practices such as prayer, meditation, or yoga. *Feminist* spirituality describes a way of life that seeks to realize the sacred by means of embodiment in female bodies and feminine ways of knowing. So what's the difference between *seeking* and *relating*? Many spiritual people today would identify themselves as seekers of God, the divine, an ultimate value, something that transcends them, a higher power, or what they would call the sacred. Such quest language tends to characterize the sacred as a goal to be reached and removes the sacred from a person's immediate experience, indicating that the divine or sacred presence has to and can be found elsewhere. This sensibility evokes a sense of a journey or life's pilgrimage upon which the seeker should be bent. Seeking can be problematic when it creates an occasion for people to understand themselves as motivated to act in ways that put them closer to that presence somewhere else rather than living the reality that such presence is already and always necessarily present.

Though it might be fun to think of oneself on an adventurous journey in life and sacred pilgrimage is a profound experience in many religious traditions all over the world, the quest motif restricts the potential for recognizing the sacred right where one is. Further, the quest metaphor also contributes to restlessness and dissatisfaction with one's own place not just metaphorically but quite literally—a very important issue that must be recognized in light of contemporary climate change and ecological crises. Part of the damage to our fragile and yet resilient planet has happened because people grew dissatisfied with their environments, having (often) depleted the resources available to them in that place. Having exploited as much of their environment as they could where they lived, many (but not all) of our ancestors, especially those whom we may think of as settlers or colonists, moved on to new places to find new resources for their sustenance and flourishing—often at the cost of local inhabitants of those places, human and animal, plant and mineral.

Nowadays, this kind of movement to new places is even easier to accomplish with our cars, airplanes, and trains, and yet until more sophisticated technologies evolve and we do a better job relating to the bioregions we already inhabit, this tendency will take a toll on the planet. Even our programs of aerospace exploration draw from this troubling tendency in human nature to exploit a habitat for one's own purposes. Consider: how would our world be different if we were more like trees and took seriously our valuing of rootedness in communities of origin and in place? Would our planetary home be as damaged as it now is? Would our actions have made it necessary for climate refugees to seek asylum in places removed from their homelands? One might argue that we are not meant to be like trees, but I hope to show throughout this book that we have more in common with all our neighbors (not just human) on this planet than we might realize. Our lives seen in continuity with theirs offer wisdom for more responsible and holistic living in earthly community. While it is true that human life expresses itself with special gifts of insight and imagination, as we become more aware of our creaturely continuity with other nonhuman or other-than-human life-forms, our relationship with the sacred as the source and sustainer of all life deepens. Further, as we discern and experience our interdependence and commonality, this new understanding may help us foster habits of gratitude and reverence for the various life-forms with whom we share a planetary home—these beings whose participation in sourcing and sustaining our own lives renders their beings sacred too.

As human beings, we, like plants, grow from small beginnings that are seedlike as we are nourished by all the things our whole being needs to change over time; certain aspects of our being then blossom in the sense of coming into visibility with the potential to bear fruit; and finally, our lives offer fruit like some plants for others who are nourished by our being. Maybe you have heard the phrase "bloom where you are planted" to indicate a certain focus on the sustainable use and appreciation of material and sociospiritual provisions forming your context. This phrase also expresses the importance of the continuity of human and plant lives. We have more in common with many of the creatures with whom we share life on planet Earth than we realize—so much so that the way we talk about ourselves reveals a lot about how deeply we recognize this commonality or whether we are not aware of it at all. Practice listening for these ways of talking and how they reflect awareness or lack of awareness of our connection with the natural world.[1] For instance, our language reflects our increasing entanglement with digital and mechanistic technologies. I often catch myself before I use metaphors of "recharging one's battery" or "unplugging" to speak of relaxation or before I use the metaphor of "feedback" in the classroom to speak of critical reflection exchanged between people, not wanting to reinforce the increasing sense of the continuity of human life with that of machines—or that which is artificial and manufactured by humans. It is important to notice how much our language reflects our evolving experience of life and human identity.

Even though language is vitally important to understand and to manage effectively, fundamental to spirituality and ecospirituality is a focus on *experience* rather than words that describe, explain, or justify beliefs. Though this book will be full of words and even words about what I believe, these words are meant to indicate how experience informs understanding and how experience may be intentionally engaged in order to shape a person's life. This is the fundamental purpose and outcome of spiritual practices with an intention to foster and attend to the sacred in one's relationship with the natural world. Such practices are also known as *ecospiritual practices*. These practices help us engage and deepen our relationship with the natural world as sacred first and only then interpret our experience yielding knowledge; these practices help us grow in awareness, acceptance, and appreciation of others, our earthly home, all who belong in our shared earthly community, and ultimately, the sacred.

Religion and ecology (or religious ecology), ecotheology, and ecomysticism are other fields of study and practice that bring together some of the same issues fundamental to ecospirituality.[2] How ecospirituality differs from religion and ecology and from ecotheology, however, is its focus on experience within the natural world being considered sacred and the holding in tension of our human identity as belonging within the natural world and enlivened in the ways other living beings are as well. Llewellyn Vaughan-Lee made this distinction well when he wrote, "In recent years there has been much work in the field of religious ecology, offering a scriptural or theological basis to an ecological approach: for example, the idea of 'stewardship' or 'trusteeship' in the Bible and the Qur'an. 'Spiritual ecology' [or ecospirituality] articulates the need for an ecological approach *founded in spiritual awareness rather than religious belief*."[3]

I will return to this notion of spiritual awareness below. The distinction, however, between ecotheology and ecospirituality arises, as well, from the idea Vaughan-Lee shares. While theology tends to be talking or thinking about (*logos*) God (*theo*) and ecotheology contains this discourse and reflection within attention to the natural world, such talk or thinking can be abstract and even differ radically from how a person actually lives—experiencing and practicing attitudes of gratitude, respect, and love for the natural world, the sacred, or God. Those working in the field of spirituality studies explore experience, especially that of people concerned with recognizing and affirming the presence of God and the sacred in all places. This is not to say that theologians are not themselves engaged in experiential work and interpreting their own and others' experiences in order to better understand and thus talk about God; but typically, theological discourse has had to do with articulating axioms of belief about God that may or may not relate to a person's experience of the sacred. Sometimes, these thinkers jump too hastily to conversations about God or the sacred rather than relishing the actual experience that may or may not be communicable in the first place.

Many of us have hiked to the top of a mountain or into a forest and felt some sense of presence, an amplification or humbling of our own being, or even just wonder and awe start up within us. This palpable sense of the sacred helps us experience and understand ourselves as integral parts of a whole. We may feel invited to talk about this experience with others but with a shared understanding that the experience itself creates change in us, actualizing our vital relationships with others without our needing or being able to explain what is happening. This deferral of explanation may seem frustrating—as if we are unnecessarily mystifying a quite common experience—but it is an inevitable aspect of religious and philosophical traditions that contain a *mystical* dimension. Such traditions affirm experiences of feeling at one with the sacred in a manner that exceeds conceptual understanding or description. Ecomysticism is a discourse parallel to ecospirituality that centers the natural world as the site of sacred encounter and affirms a person's experience of loving union within the context of the natural world.

Both ecospirituality and ecomysticism focus on experience. How ecospirituality differs from ecomysticism is in its focus on holding in tension the interconnectedness and relationality of all creation, without collapse of individual parts to accomplish union. Though "individual" can be a problematic word when it indicates individualism as an isolating feature of contemporary life, the word really indicates indivisibility—that is, the inability to be divided. We, as human creatures, are individuals, meaning we are indivisibly composed of parts: our minds, our hearts, our bodies, our emotions. These all come together to form a unity while each part remains uniquely itself and participatory in creating the whole of us. The same is true of each one of us within the communities we help form and the natural world we live in. While ecomysticism would describe experience of union with the natural world as a potential collapse of distinction, ecospirituality would maintain the uniqueness of parts that nevertheless together form a whole. An example of this distinction is Terry Tempest Williams's quotation at the beginning of this book. She writes, "Whatever I know as a woman about spirituality I have learned from my body encountering Earth. Soul and soil are not separate. Neither are mind and spirit, nor water and tears."[4] She does not say these things are the same—though the chemical composition of our own bodily fluids does uncannily resemble fluids found in the natural world. What she does say is that these things are not separate. There is an important relationship between them in the encounter of similarity and difference, and holding these similarities and differences in tension and celebrating them is the work of those in ecospirituality studies and of those engaging ecospiritual practices.

Ecospirituality's inclusion of *spirit* also indicates an important point of differentiation from ecomysticism. *Spirit* may seem a very religious word and concept, but in the context of ecospirituality, it has very material, though perhaps intangible, dimensions, functioning as the enlivening agent or energy or depth dimension throughout and within creation, ourselves included, and facilitating a shared phenomenon of lived experience that permits union but also celebrates communion, or kin relationships between distinct forms of life.

WHAT YOU WILL FIND IN THIS BOOK

The first chapters in this book cover background in the Christian spiritual tradition, beginning with a chapter on particular experiences of belonging within the natural world and relating with the sacred as expressed in the Bible, or Judeo-Christian Scriptures. In this chapter, we will explore the natural imagery that biblical writers used to explain their experiences of God and their self-understanding of how spiritual change happens. From the very beginning of these chapters that offer a grounding in Christian spiritual history, we will see that people of faith in the Judeo-Christian traditions understood and celebrated an important continuity between themselves as humans and the rest of creation, even while they grappled with divine authorization to exercise dominion over creation as human beings made "in the image of God" (Gen 1:26–27). Understanding the influence of the Bible's cosmological narratives—those stories that tell of beginnings—and other biblical values on contemporary culture will help us determine whether or not to agree with critics who claim Christianity's anthropocentrism, or human-centered perspective, is largely responsible for ecological crises today.

Following what the Gospels tell of Jesus periodically retreating to the wilderness to pray (Mark 1:35, Luke 4:42), Christians have regularly regarded the natural world as a site of divine encounter. Chapter 2 describes a fourth-century movement of Christians who valued the wilderness experience—particularly the desert wilderness—as formative of their spiritual lives and as enabling the important fasting and prayer practices they engaged as they grew in their awareness of God's presence with them in their solitude and in their various communities. I connect these ancient exemplars of life in balance with the natural world to examples of movements today that may build on their wisdom or innovate with themes that yet resonate with the Christian desert tradition. Chapter 3 looks at two figures who drew their understandings of self and God from their experience of the natural world in a way that has proved exemplary for the emergence of ecospirituality in the twenty-first century: Francis of Assisi and Hildegard of Bingen. Each of these figures is introduced as focusing on kinship and the restorative dimensions of human relationship with the natural world that remain vital to our own experiences of the natural world today. Chapter 4 marks the end of this historical foundation in the Christian spiritual tradition by introducing two modern figures, Wendell Berry and Thomas Berry (unrelated, though they share the same last name). Though it may seem problematic to focus on the contributions to ecospirituality of two such homogeneous figures as these—both white males and both American—their contributions diverge in the sense of being oriented toward ethical land use (Wendell) and cosmology (Thomas). Without disowning their contributions to ecospirituality, we will examine them with respect, using the fact that they are two white men to alert us to the ongoing privilege involved in allowing certain people to experience and explore their experience of the sacred earth more readily than many others.

With this foundation in place, we will see why expressions of renewed interest in creation care are showing up amid our compromised living habitats today—we will see what ideas, what *seeds* were sown in the ground of history, narrowly conceived, for speaking of God, human identity, human experience, and human responsibility. Though my perspective derives from my own identity as one formed within the Judeo-Christian tradition, the influence of these traditions has become global by the twenty-first century (for good and for bad), and much of what is described in these opening chapters is invitational for all readers to reflect on, whether they identify as belonging within these traditions or not. My hope is that some of the ideas in these chapters resonate with your own experience and values, whatever your own cultural context.

Chapters 5 and 6 explore ecospiritual practice. Experiential learning and engagement are of primary importance in spirituality studies. In fact, when I was a student, one of my teachers spoke of my own experience as another book I needed to research just as much as the texts of Augustine, Julian of Norwich, or Dietrich Bonhoeffer. This approach is no different in the area of ecospirituality. We learn about our relationship with the sacred by nurturing that relationship and listening to our experience of the sacred, in addition to the more academic or literary work of reading and interpreting written texts that are accounts of other people's reflections on their experiences of the sacred. These texts, of course, expand our awareness of what is possible, but they may also limit our awareness; for this reason, it is important that we learn to attend to and value our own experience and bring it into dialogue with what we learn from and with others. It can be hard to make time for deliberate engagement with the natural world, but that is what many of the practices found at the end of each chapter in this book urge us to do.

The particular ecospiritual practices discussed in these chapters spring from global contexts. While I often favor the potential in Catholic spiritual practices because they are most familiar to me and can often be made relevant and inspiring with slight modification for those lacking or resisting religious grounding, there are many ways that spiritual practices across religious traditions are being "greened" in order to meet the needs of the members of faith communities today. To green a spiritual practice merely means to foreground its existing eco-friendly dimensions or to revise the practice while respecting the reasons the practice evolved in the first place so that it contains eco-friendly dimensions. What do I mean by "eco-friendly dimensions"? I mean a practice with eco-friendly dimensions would not be an occasion for inflicting ecological damage or severing our relationship with the sacred; rather, it would enable us to foster recognition of, respect for, and celebration of our relatedness with the sacred in the context of the natural world. If we have grown distant from our awareness of being in relationship with others, an ecospiritual practice or greened spiritual practice would restore that awareness. This experiential grounding might lead to a person's changed ethical orientation and to making new commitments to safeguard the well-being of others—commitments that might permeate one's whole life, such as the choices one makes about the food one eats or the clothing one wears or the activities one engages in. Sometimes, as well, these practices themselves might emerge from an ethical sensibility and be lived out in a mundane manner quite apart from the deliberate periods of prayer, meditation, or religious ritual that seem most obvious forms of spiritual practice. Chapter 5 describes spiritual practices from Hinduism, Christianity, Judaism, Islam, and Buddhism. These practices are transformative in the basic forms they have been practiced for centuries, and yet when greened, they accrue even more significance and transformative potential for those who engage them today. Seeing how these specific practices are greened will model opportunities for your own investigation into practices you may be familiar with that could be greened as well.

Next, we will look at practices that have dimensions of traditional practice but are a bit more experimental and novel in the way they have been adjusted to meet the needs of both those who do and those who do not identify as religious. Many of the practices in this chapter, just as in the chapter on greening traditional practices, may feel comfortable to anyone and express values an environmentally and socially conscious person might feel. These ecospiritual practices offer opportunities to restore attention to and to nurture something that we all have—regardless of tradition or lack of religious tradition—by virtue of being human: a relationship with the sacred or with that which gives and sustains life. In fact, the foundational quality of these ecospiritual practices is the ground for interreligious dialogue and the reviving of religious traditions that may be in decline. As religions are greened in the ways they can be practiced, they attract adherents and the respect of outsiders who can better understand one another across sectarian divisions because of shared experience of the sacred in the natural world. In this way the apostle Paul's words that in the early Christian faith community, "there is no longer Jew or Greek, there is no longer slave or free, there is no longer male and female; for all of you are one in Christ Jesus" (Gal 3:28), could be greened to include, "There is no longer Jew or Christian or Muslim or Hindu or Buddhist or SBNR (Spiritual But Not Religious); for all of you are one in your concern for the earth."

The ecospiritual practices in this book are not meant to alienate any reader who does or does not identify as religious. I am reminded of a quip made by a meditation teacher that just as drinking coffee does not make a person Hawaiian, Costa Rican, or Ethiopian, depending on where one's coffee beans originate, neither does meditating or doing yoga or praying make you Buddhist, Hindu, or Jewish. There is a lot more that goes into self-identifiers such as belief systems, faith commitments, and communities of belonging that facilitate a person's self-understanding as a particular kind of religious person. The wealth of practices and rituals that help humans make meaning of their experience is available to the Earth human community in ways never before possible due to electronic communications and the increasing access to information and innovation such communications make possible. My hope is that the ecospiritual practices described in this middle section of the book will spark your curiosity, that you will try them and discover how they might renew and nurture your relationship with the sacred.

After reviewing major world religions and innovative greening of spiritual practice, we will look at Indigenous spiritual practices rooted in gratitude and contemplative awareness that spring from centuries of living in close relationship with the natural world. Recovering respect and reverence and offering larger space in our settler communities for Indigenous resurgence is an important movement of our time, and chapter 7's attention to particular practices is meant not to suggest their appropriation as further colonization but rather to help us all see more clearly the values and practices that were marginalized by settler tendencies and that might be rewoven into all of our attempts to become more indigenous to our places, which Robin Wall Kimmerer defines as living in a way that expresses care for the future of the place where we live and those who will live there after we do. The experiences of those in communities most ancient and still thriving despite tremendous loss offer wisdom to the worldwide community and give us energy, too, to create the kind of world we need and that would best contribute to the flourishing of all members of the Earth community.

In the final chapter, I describe interdisciplinary areas that have combined some essential aspects of their own focus of engagement with ecology and, furthermore, with ecospirituality. Such areas as ecojustice and ecofeminism provide points of contact with the work that ecospirituality makes possible and have important implications for personal and social transformation. Some people have called the movement to a more socially engaged spirituality a "second wave spirituality," and that might be one way to characterize what ecospirituality contributes in being focused on bringing an individual into renewed contact with their depth dimension through engagement of the sacred in the natural world, not only to enhance their own well-being but to contribute to the well-being of others.

Tracing movements of ecospirituality with metaphors of seed to harvest as a framework—or trellis, if you will—for this book provides a foil to the typical spiritual quest or journey imagery so common to Christian and other religious traditions. Quest imagery assumes a heroic figure intent on transformation from an essentially dissatisfied-with-the-self position, intent on moving the lesser self to a better self through deeds of valor and conquest. While that imagery may motivate many people, it also does a lot of damage when cultivating a sense of inadequacy and inauthenticity in the self and a sense of the urgent need to move elsewhere in order to access one's deeper or truer self. This tendency has damaged the facility of folks to remain in place, to let their metaphorical roots run deep, and even to recognize the sacred about and within them at all times, regardless of their location. The pervasive presence of the sacred is a fundamental axiom of ecospirituality and allows us to sit uncomfortably with past representations of God as transcendent and also with one's best self as transcendent to oneself (resulting in self-alienation rather than self-formation). Deepened engagement with these ideas throughout the book will, I hope, yield a harvest in you, the reader—one ripe in meaning for yourself, providing sustenance for your ongoing growth and for that of others.

My hope is that a true harvest from this book is your reaping benefit from your engagement not only with the ideas and resources this book provides but also in investigating your own experience and taking time to consider how important the natural world is in forming your own identity. If you have never considered your relationship to the natural world as spiritual, this book is for you! And if you have always considered your relationship to the natural world as spiritual, this book is for you, too! We are beginning together a season of growth that I hope continues beyond this book, rooting you in the communities, social and natural, that best facilitate your flourishing.

Questions for Reflection and Discussion

- How would you explain the importance of the spiritual in everyday life?
- What is the language you use for God or the sacred?
- What is the story of your relationship with the natural world?
- Do you prefer the metaphor of spiritual journey or spiritual growth? Why?
- What does your life look like when you are flourishing?

Suggested Ecospiritual Practices

Begin spending regular and intentional time outside without any agenda or expectation as to what will happen there. Go into the outdoors without use of electronic devices. Take out your earbuds, keep your phone in a pocket. Resist taking pictures, even if surrounded by beauty. Be present with whatever you find in a park, in your neighborhood, in a backyard, on a balcony, or near an open window where you can breathe deeply of fresh air. Take enough time for your sensual perception to sharpen and to become aware of your interior landscape: Do you feel awe or wonder, fear or loneliness, boredom or frustration when in the presence of the natural world? What is the source of those feelings? Consider this an invitation to grow in self-awareness and in courage to acknowledge feelings that might be pleasurable or might be unpleasant.

Meditate with and reflect on poetry that speaks to your heart. A new literary subgenre of poetry called *ecopoetics* consists of poems that evoke transformation in the reader, especially when expressing recognition of the ecological changes and challenges we are experiencing in the twenty-first century. Christian Wiman claimed that reading poetry enables us to more fully inhabit our lives and world; further, he claimed "that if we more fully inhabit these things, we might be less apt to destroy both."[5] That is a powerful statement! What would it mean for you to more fully inhabit your life? To more fully inhabit your world? Though poetry can be difficult to read and understand, its ambivalent nature renders it perfect for slow reading, deep reflection, and honest discussion. Many chapters in this book will contain suggestions of poems you might read meditatively as a part of your ecospiritual practice. I suggest reading Jane Hirshfield's "Tree" because it conveys an image familiar to many of us who live in close proximity to one another.[6] This poem asks us to consider which life—tree or human—is encroaching upon the other? Which life might be better off staying in its place? Do we have to choose? What does it mean to choose? Consider this an invitation to identify what might be tapping at your life as you begin the reading of this book.

For Further Reading

Claiming Earth as Common Ground: The Ecological Crisis through the Lens of Faith by Andrea Cohen-Kiener (SkyLight Paths, 2009)

Nature as Spiritual Practice by Steven Chase (Eerdmans, 2011)

Sacred Longings: The Ecological Spirit and Global Culture by Mary Grey (Fortress, 2004)

Science and Spiritual Practices: Transformative Experiences and Their Effects on Our Bodies, Brains, and Health by Rupert Sheldrake (Counterpoint, 2018)

Second Wave Spirituality: Passion for Peace, Passion for Justice by Chris Saade (North Atlantic, 2014)

CHAPTER ONE
Biblical Ecospirituality

As the primary manifestation of the divine, the natural world is the primary sacred scripture and the primary sacred community. There could be no verbal scriptures unless first there were the cosmic scriptures.
—Thomas Berry, *The Sacred Universe: Earth, Spirituality, and Religion in the Twenty-First Century*

Biblical scholars, people of faith, and others read the Bible for various reasons. One reason is to find and understand stories that teach what it means to be human and to be in relationships—with God, with others both within and outside one's community, and with the natural world. A new method of reading and interpreting the Bible is emerging within the field of biblical studies that is useful for engaging the Bible, sacred texts in other wisdom traditions, and even secular literary works across disciplines. The principles involved in this process of interpretation suggest a new orientation we might adopt and employ toward differing aspects of our lives inside and even outside educational settings, including pondering legislation, business practices, or health care policy. Further, many passages in the Bible foster creation care and ethical attention to the plight of the marginalized who, in our own day, are increasingly those most affected by aspects of climate change, not to mention all the animals, plants, mountains, lakes, forests, plains, and glaciers so affected.

The Bible is an anthology of books written by different people over a period of many centuries. For that reason, biblical writings express different positions taken by different authors on how they understand God telling them to act in relation to one another and the land. Some passages, early in the Bible, tell of creation's origins and explain human identity, experience, and purpose in relationship with the rest of creation. Other passages in the Bible draw from prophetic voices and use imagery of flourishing plant and animal relationships to indicate conditions and experiences of social and environmental justice. Some passages even explore the creaturely continuity between humans and animals as a matter of humans' "inner animality."[1] Later passages in the text, which are important for Christians, demonstrate Jesus's sensitivity to the natural world as he taught using imagery of seeds and plants, sheep and camels to diagnose relationship problems and to restore individual, social, and even ecological well-being. Each of these passages from various sections of the Bible provide "seeds" of insight for understanding what is possible when people encounter the sacred in the natural world. Though these seeds are biblical and may for that reason be thought to be foundational only for Jewish and Christian doctrinal understanding, here the focus is on how these scriptural seeds explore the potential for human engagement and experience of the natural world as sacred more widely.

While many people may not consider themselves biblically literate—even those members of a community that roots its proclamation of faith in the Bible—most cultures have nevertheless been affected in some way or another by how our forebears read and interpreted the Judeo-Christian Scriptures and how these forebears drew their own self-understanding and understanding of God and of the natural world from these sacred texts. Sometimes, these connections are not explicit but implicit in worldviews that derive from biblical author-ity, even in cultures that would hesitate to grant the Bible overt authority. How we manage the impact of biblical worldviews on our own behavior and communities is up to us and how our collaborative process of engagement with the Bible and biblical ideas and values unfolds.

The famous ecotheologian (or geologian, as he preferred to be called[2]) Thomas Berry, whose words form an epigraph of this chapter, advised laying aside the Bible for a time until we recover a sense of the universe as the primary revelation of the sacred. Certainly, not all biblical scholars, rabbis, priests, or ministers have agreed with Berry. They would be out of a job if they did! Instead, certain biblical scholars see our devastated environment—with animal extinctions and biodiversity loss, pollution and global warming—as a wake-up call to renew critical suspicion of the Bible when it seems to justify resource depletion and wanton disregard for the creatures with whom we share our planetary home. Such biblical scholars see this time of ecological crisis as a wake-up call to also begin reading the Bible anew to appreciate more fully its themes of creation care, interconnectedness, and ecojustice. But consider what Berry wanted to accomplish: What would happen to us if we did set aside some of our devotional engagement with texts such as the Bible and the influential ideas we seem to have drawn from them within the church setting or even at home and instead engaged more memorably and favorably with our natural settings? Would we be better able to care for these places if we experienced them as sacred in the way a cathedral, grotto, shrine, temple, synagogue, or mosque is understood as sacred space?

To return to Berry's insight about the usefulness of setting aside the Bible for a time, it might seem that many of us have set it aside, as many no longer consider it authoritative for their own lives or ethical commitments. Nevertheless, it has had an incalculable effect on many people's worldviews and actions. For instance, in my own context of living in the United States, the settlers of this country regularly drew on biblical imagery of occupation of the "Promised Land" to justify their own actions, which included hostile and lethal interactions with Indigenous peoples and extractive and exploitative behavior toward the land.[3] A landmark essay by Lynn White in 1967 argued that Christianity bears the heaviest burden of all religions for having caused the ecological crises we face today because of the influence of Christian traditions on global cultures and Christianity's anthropocentric, or human-centered, perspective and biased promotion of humans acting on their own interests at the expense of others.[4] Rather than despair over this accusation, however, many Christians and biblical scholars have sought to offer a corrective to what they see as a *misuse* of the Bible to legitimate exploitative behavior among people and between people and the rest of creation. This corrective in biblical studies has taken the form of a liberation lens at times and a "green lens" at others that one can apply when reading the Bible.[5] As noted earlier, I believe this green lens and the principles and procedure involved in using it are really important and can be applied to other texts and contexts.

The first step of using this green lens in biblical studies is *suspicion*. This means reading with the assumption that any text, biblical or otherwise, inevitably displays anthropocentric bias because the text was produced by humans formed within a particular human sociopolitical context. This means reading with a certain amount of skepticism that the text can, by virtue of its limited perspective, tell the whole story inclusive of other, more-than-human perspectives. Such anthropocentricism is not necessarily a bad thing on its own, but it should be named and accounted for, especially when it becomes a means of distorting our understanding and justifying behavior harmful to other members of our global family.

The second step of using this green lens involves *identification*. This means taking advantage of our privileged identity as humans as critically reflective and imaginative thinkers and sentient beings and identifying with the perspective of other-than-human actors in the text whose stories might have been told differently than the human narrators' or human editors' versions of the story. Being able to empathize and enter creatively into the experience of another is the peculiar gift of humanity—as far as we know—and biblical scholars using this green lens have encouraged each other to use this gift in their scholarship. Sometimes, this creativity produces work that does not look like ordinary scholarship—when it involves giving voice to another using the genre of a lyric poem, for instance. Nevertheless, the legitimate use of creativity in one's scholarship is meant to underscore how essentially creative *all* our readings and interpretations of the Bible and other literatures are.

A final step of using this green lens is *retrieval*. This means retrieving the wisdom that might derive from a biblical passage once we acknowledge our anthropocentric bias and imaginatively identify with the text's other-than-human actors to provide a wider scope for the narrative. This process applied to biblical and other texts can help us shift our worldview to one more expansive in consideration of the others with whom we share our planetary home.[6]

Biblical scholars have also formulated principles to frame their understanding of the natural world in the biblical text and in their own contemporary contexts. These principles loosely relate to the three steps of using a green lens to read the Bible. For instance, tied to *suspicion* of anthropocentric bias are the principles of intrinsic *value* and the principle of *purpose*, meaning we acknowledge that every part of creation has value and purpose quite independent of the value or purpose humans might assign these parts of creation.

Tied to the step of *identification* with more-than-human actors in the text are the principles of *interconnectedness* and *mutual custodianship*, meaning we as human members of the Earth community have the capacity through our understanding of the fact of our interdependence with all creation to intuitively try to imagine what others might experience. For instance, ethologists, who study animal behavior, are understanding more fully how we share certain emotions such as fear, grief, and satisfaction with other animals. The shared experience of pursuing an end—of desire, in fact—means we know a lot more about the perspectives of others on Earth than we might otherwise realize or even like to admit. It is easier to think, like Descartes, that the crying of an animal being slaughtered is a mere mechanical reflex; it might help us eat our hamburgers with less guilt. But is it true? Many people say *no*. Just as we would not like to be kept in an overcrowded pen, have our young taken from us prematurely, be overfed and over-medicated, so many of the creatures we treat in this manner resist, indicating a profound responsibility for each other that we would do well to honor. Further, our earthly home cares and provides for us by way of air, water, food, and other essential needs for which we cannot possibly pay. Human responsibility entails then a caretaking function, but this is not a one-way street where humans consider themselves the sole distributors of goods or benefits to others. Rather, as humans regard themselves as vulnerably interdependent with other parts of creation, this necessitates our thinking carefully and thoroughly about how we relate to the natural world and when it may be right or wrong to privilege our own interests, just because we have the (limited) power to do so.

Finally, the step of *retrieval* in the process of applying a green lens to a text fleshes out principles of *voice* and *resistance*, meaning that as we engage the Bible (and other texts) using a green lens, we "hear" more clearly the voice of other-than-human nature, and we even hear the voice of these other-than-human actors in our global and cosmic shared stories as speaking with resistance to human projects of domination and exploitation. These resistant voices speak a perspective important for us to retrieve in the process of restoring our identity and roles in the Earth community as a whole.

Whether or not we follow Thomas Berry's advice and intentionally set the Bible "aside" (and are even capable of doing this in terms of negating or mitigating its past influence on our own mindset and the mindset of others today), we might consider Berry's goal. He especially wanted to emphasize how fundamental and essential the natural world is as our primary context—our primarily revelatory context—meaning the natural world reveals something really important about the sacred, or God, that some people of faith have only thought the Bible capable of doing. thought the Bible capable of doing. Further, the natural world is our first occasion of understanding that there *is* something sacred. Berry not only called the universe the primary revelation of the sacred but also defined the sacred for us as that which evokes wonder. This, indeed, is primary, and perhaps it does take setting aside a great number of things besides the Bible to come to an experiential realization of the universe's primacy in our concerns and in our coming to understand anything at all about who God is as Creator or, if God language does not seem comfortable to describe this aspect of human experience, in our coming to understand what truly is the sacred as life-giving.

GENESIS:
"IN THE BEGINNING . . ."

Cosmologies or creation stories are important in different traditions because they not only provide a framework for understanding how humans and everything else have come to exist in the first place but also *activate* a human's behavior as that person responds to their understanding of their identity in the world. Surprisingly, there is not just one biblical account of creation in the opening chapters of the Bible, but two. They each emphasize different aspects of human identity and divine identity, given the differing perspectives of the original communities of storytellers, authors, and editors responsible for composing and saving the material. If you think of what you know about these first creation stories, you probably know a lot. You have probably heard the names Adam, Eve, and the garden of Eden before. They have entered global popular culture; as one small example, I cite the name of my favorite bakery, "Back to Eden." You can probably guess what the bakery owners are trying to express about their own baked goods in calling their shop by this name, right? You may also remember that a snake appears in one of the biblical creation accounts. And a tree or two. Whether or not you know the details of the stories, they have affected the way many of us think about ourselves in the world.

The first creation account explains not only how everything came to be but also why humans organize time into a week of seven days and why Jews and Christians celebrate a day of holy rest at the end of the week. God is seen as setting a divine precedent in resting from the work of creation, so humans understand themselves as permitted and even beholden to do so as well. Later biblical legislation drew on this gift of rest when extending it to other parts of creation such as animals and the land. This emphasis on rest in the first creation account is meant to activate human behavior in response to a specific understanding of human identity, and it coincides with the intent of the Jewish authors and editors who wanted to emphasize the importance of keeping the Sabbath, especially during times when it was difficult to do so. Doing so was an important identity marker in a society that preferred the Jewish people to assimilate into non-Jewish culture.

The second creation account evokes human universals of experience, rather than the Israelite-specific context, in attempting to explain some fundamentals of human experience, such as why work is often so difficult, why women often experience pain when they give birth, and why many humans fear snakes and many snakes fear humans.[7] This second creation story is meant to resonate with the reader's experience, explaining otherwise inexplicable phenomena of human experience while providing a warning to the reader about the dire consequences of disobeying God, again relevant to specific readers who might have seemed in danger of assimilation into foreign cultures and of disregard of their own culturally specific practices.

Not only do the biblical creation stories present human identity and implicitly prescribed actions in different ways; they also present God as Creator in different ways. In the first creation account, God is presented as all-powerful when God merely commands that things come into existence and they do. Sequentially, through days of creating, all that is comes to be, and significantly, we find that biodiversity is built into these days of creation when the text attaches the words "of every kind" repeatedly to the plants and animals created (Gen 1:11–12, 21, 24–25). It is as if everything that would ever come into existence had its seeds in these ancient primogenitors. In addition, God is not the only creator in the first account of creation. Rather, the earth cocreates with God while exhibiting exemplary obedience to God's commands. When God says, for instance, "Let the earth bring forth . . ." (Gen 1:24), the earth is responsive and *does* bring forth. Furthermore, everything that is brought forth is repeatedly affirmed as *good*. The storytellers of this tradition wanted to counteract any suspicion to the contrary. This ancient account of creation is a wonderful expression of the natural world as fundamentally generative and in relationship with a sacred source of generativity whom many know as God. We can assess this expression of the natural world's fecundity against our own experience of seeing how all plants and animals, humans included, contain reproductive processes that continue to yield life in ways responsive to their own natures. Religious people might understand this process as initiated by divine decree, inscribed into the very nature of all things. Many ecotheologians emphasize as well that nature, ourselves included, was not a static entity at this originating moment; these ecotheologians speak of *cosmogenesis* to mean that creation is ongoing and occurs pervasively throughout the context of the universe rather than static and confined to a single origin of human becoming in time and space within our own experience of planet Earth. We live in a vibrantly material world, ever forming and transforming, and we are cocreators in processes of change even as we ourselves are created in an ongoing manner, not just at our moment of conception or birth individually or as a species. The sacred quality of this ongoing creation constitutes a new and exciting understanding of who God is and how God remains involved in the ongoing work of creation, an understanding that permits people with scientific and religious outlooks to begin to use language together that they understand and affirm.

In the second creation account, an anthropomorphic or personified God appears in closer contact to and as an intimate presence with humans while walking with them through the garden that God has been pictured as actually planting to be their home. This is a God who is willing to get God's hands dirty! Indeed, this God seems very hands-on in forming the first human being from the very ground and breathing into this being's nostrils (Gen 2:7). This picture of human creation is very important in actualizing an understanding of subsequent human identity and behavior as continuous with earthly life. The human in this second creation account is shaped from the actual ground: the Hebrew word for this human creature (*adam*) bears a significant resemblance to the Hebrew word for the earthly ground (*adamah*). This resemblance suggests fundamental interconnectedness.

In this second creation account, we are reminded that the first humans had an intimate rapport with God, with animals, with plants, and with the natural setting in which they lived. This harmony is disrupted by what is represented as disobedient behavior. The fracture between humans and their natural home is seen by some theologians as fundamental to human experience. The juxtaposition of how humans regard the trees of the garden demonstrates this disruption to the human experience of the sacred in the natural world. Just as the repetitious statements about the goodness of creation in the first creation account are meant to activate a future faith community's awareness of the goodness of creation within which they live, the narrator of the second creation story tells us that God made trees to grow in the garden of Eden that were "pleasant to the sight and good for food" (Gen 2:9). Later we find that one of the humans looks upon the trees' fruit and the narrator tellingly switches the position of the attributes given the tree earlier; the tree is seen as "good for food, and . . . a delight to the eyes" (Gen 3:6). Here we see the troubling tendency of humans—with their anthropocentric bias—to prioritize their own use of creation rather than to celebrate its intrinsic value and purposeful beauty quite independent of the way it might supply humans with needed sustenance. This move in the biblical text indicates an important shift, and though it is not often focused on as the moment of *sin*—that moment comes later when the fruit is actually consumed and the humans try to cover up their act when God questions them about it—the change in perspective demonstrates a kind of orientation that would become habitual and lead to the devastating ecological crises we experience today. These creation stories actualize the realities to which they point. It is up to us to read them now with enough attention to see how they function to influence our thinking about ourselves and others, so we can regulate their authoritative place in our communities. Retrieving a sense of creation's goodness and of our own interconnectedness as beings whose vital substance resembles that of other parts of creation from which our whole being is created—dust and stardust, as physicists say—offers us the best of these originating biblical creation stories about human identity and responsibility and asks us to consider how well we agree with and act upon an understanding of creation as good and ourselves as vitally connected with the natural world.

PROPHETS AND PEACEABLE KIN-DOMS

The Bible starts with an image of a garden in the opening chapters of Genesis and concludes with images of a new city of God (Jerusalem) in which greenspace in the form of fertile trees and a river are important dimensions. In between these opening and closing images of the Bible, there are other writers who use natural imagery to speak of ecosystems flourishing—as a metaphor certainly for human social flourishing but also as an important indicator of what is required in order to facilitate human flourishing: the human and natural are interconnected, so social and environmental justice go hand in hand. Significantly, most of the Bible's prophetic texts emerge from a historical period when the Jewish people were dislocated from land they understood to be their God-given home. This dislocation from land constituted their primary experience of grievance and sorrow, and their primary hopes for recovery of a sacred connection to God, to their land, and to their faith community emerged from this dislocation. They understood themselves to be covenanted with God through faithfulness to God's laws mediated through relationships with one another (constituting social justice) and with the land (constituting ecojustice).

Perhaps the most famous of the prophetic imagery involving the Earth community is the prophet Isaiah's peaceable kingdom, in which animals and humans coexist harmoniously. This imagery constitutes an invigorating vision of what might happen were the Jewish people to recommit to their covenants of interconnectedness and mutual custodianship that formed a basis for their self-understanding. Isaiah writes that in that hoped-for reality,

> The wolf shall live with the lamb,
> the leopard shall lie down with the kid,
> the calf and the lion and the fatling together,
> and a little child shall lead them.
> The cow and the bear shall graze,
> their young shall lie down together;
> and the lion shall eat straw like the ox.

The nursing child shall play over the hole of the asp,
and the weaned child shall put its hand on the adder's den.
   (Isa 11:6–8)

Painters throughout history have used this biblical passage as a subject for their paintings—it is wildly effective and startling to see
some of these animals' ferocity become tender in the company of
vulnerable others. Looking at any such painting, we might be drawn
in to wonder what makes it possible for such antagonisms and fears
to disappear. Isaiah's answer is the following: the restoration of commitments to creation care and social justice. Though the imagery
in this passage might express anthropocentric interests and use the
natural world to reflect human reality, the prophet seems to say
that in God's kingdom, there are meant to be no relationships of
predation, between humans or between humans and animals and
the rest of creation. Further, because the context in which human
social, political, legislative, educational, economic, and religious
communities operate is the natural world, lack of harmony in any
one of these communities and within the larger Earth community
disrupts the possibility of harmony in any other; they are all interrelated. The prophet consciously draws on garden of Eden imagery to
evoke the readers' memories of what constituted the original vision
of human cohabitation with the rest of creation. Inclusion of the
snake, in particular, indicates a healing of the rift created in the original human community with their other-than-human neighbors
and kin. No longer, in Isaiah's peaceable place, would humans fear
snakes nor snakes fear humans.

   One note about the tendency to speak of a "kingdom" as the place
God creates within which God will "reign" as "king": These are metaphors favored in the Bible to speak of God's absolute rule and the
people's fidelity to God, reflecting sociopolitical relationships in cultures the Jewish people knew and lived among. This relationship of
king and subjects was adopted at first begrudgingly by the prophet
Samuel when he reminded the people of the injustice a king might
cause in his community by virtue of an abuse of leadership. This

did happen, and Samuel's words can be understood proleptically, having been documented during a time when his words had already come true. Because abuse of power so readily happens, we might imagine that God as the perfect king emerges as a possibility to be hoped for—God as a ruler whose power and might will transcend all earthly or human possibilities of (corrupt) leadership. For some, this is an adequate metaphor pointing to that hoped-for reality, and some people of faith continue to speak of the "kingdom of God" to express the belonging to which God invites God's people. For others, this image is a dangerous metaphor that circumvents the radical nature of interconnectedness and mutual custodianship that are important principles when engaging a green lens. The metaphor of "kingdom" to speak of a community with allegiance to God as King is better spoken of as "kin-dom" in the sense that all creatures there share kinship, a familial relationship beyond their human, biological relationships.[8] This switch of metaphors that is slowly entering feminist, biblical, and ecotheological discourses also addresses the troubling tendency of associating masculine imagery with God. For instance, it probably would seem strange to those familiar with "kingdom of God" language to hear such a place referred to as the "queendom of God." That strangeness reveals to us our commitment to imagining God as masculine. Avoiding such engendering at all and suggesting a reciprocity and connection that goes beyond that of king-subject relationships, kin-dom is useful to designate the real relationships of belonging and mutual care that we and all Earth creatures share.

The prophet Hosea also draws on creation stories to describe dysfunctional and destructive behaviors he saw happening in his time. But rather than evoke an inspirational vision of what could be possible were the people to recommit to their covenants of creation care and social justice, Hosea provides a picture of creation impacted by human injustice. The opening of Hosea's writings expresses his understanding that God was transforming the Jewish people into a wilderness (Hos 2:3) because their fidelity to covenants of justice had withered. Hosea writes,

Therefore the land mourns
and all who live in it languish;
together with the wild animals
and the birds of the air,
even the fish of the sea are perishing. (Hos 4:3)

Significantly, Hosea arranges this lament of creation in a way that
mirrors the original moment of creation recounted in Genesis of
fish, birds, wild animals, and "all" beings, inclusive of humans.[9] This
undoing of creation emphasizes the destructive impact of human
social and environmental injustice in Hosea's time and can remind
us today of our own impact on the natural world. These two prophets
and their use of imagery of the natural world in their prophetic texts
emphasize the interconnectedness and mutual custodianship of the
Earth community. Just as humans understand themselves to receive
all they need to survive—such as air, food, and water—from the natural world, they also bear responsibility to care for and resist behaviors
that impoverish the natural world.

Two other prophetic writings in the Bible—presented in a storytelling mode rather than in poetic passages like Isaiah's or Hosea's—
inspire or condemn human activity. The stories of the prophets
Jonah and Daniel help us understand the sacredness of the natural
world and our own creaturely continuity with other members of the
Earth community. First, perhaps because of the fantastic dimensions
of Jonah's experience of being eaten by a large fish often pictured as a
whale and his surviving the experience, Jonah's story is one frequently
enjoyed by children in Christian Sunday schools. While Jonah was in
the belly of this whale, wondering what was going to happen to him,
he prayed in words that likely expressed the concern of many of the
Jews in exile, dislocated from land they thought God had promised
them. Jonah asked, "How shall I look again upon your holy temple?" (Jonah 2:4). Rather than complain about his condition fully,
however, Jonah expressed confidence that he would again be present
in the temple to pray someday. His readers were then able, as well,
to experience their own confidence that someday they too would

again be able to pray to God within the temple in Jerusalem. In the meantime, Jonah's experiential engagement with God through prayer occurred in the unlikeliest of places and served to teach readers that they too might engage and converse with the sacred in the unlikeliest of places—the belly of a fish. Jonah continued with these words:

> As my life was ebbing away,
> I remembered the Lord;
> and my prayer came to you,
> into your holy temple. (Jonah 2:7)

Jonah found a sacred place *within* an animal's body. This is something we are unlikely to experience ourselves, and yet the fact of his voicing a prayer from the belly of the fish lets us see this setting as a primary sacred site—as a temple of God—unusual, of course, and yet efficacious in permitting Jonah's voice to be heard by God who responded by ordering the fish to spew Jonah out. Being the exemplary creature with a relationship to God of the fish's own and about which we might be curious, the fish obeyed. Having cared for Jonah's vulnerable body in the swirling waters of the sea, the fish restrained the appetites that might have been natural to the fish's bodily experience and obeyed God. In a similar manner, readers were invited to consider how they too might be held and cared for by creation, even in places seemingly treacherous from which they may voice praise and lament, and to respond to the sacred enveloping world in a manner that reciprocates such care.

The opposite situation of inhabiting an animal body happens to the Babylonian king Nebuchadnezzar in a story told in the book of Daniel. Rather than enter into the life of the animal in the way that Jonah did, this unjust king discovered the animal within himself as a way back to himself. The story tells that this unjust king had a terrible nightmare about seeming to be transformed into an animal, and the prophet Daniel was at hand to help him understand what the nightmare meant. The first four chapters that open the book of Daniel unfold as a transformative moment in Nebuchadnezzar's life when he realized what Eric Meyer calls Nebuchadnezzar's "inner animality."[10] Critiquing traditional interpretations of Nebuchadnezzar's condition of being transformed into an animal as punishment (implying that animals are bad) or insanity (implying that animals lack intelligence or understanding), Meyer argues that Nebuchadnezzar's transformation can be charted through movements of disregard for God (Dan 1); recognition of God (Dan 2); fearful reverence of God (Dan 3); and finally, worship, personal devotion, and even remediation of past injustice (Dan 4). This transformation of his character reached its culmination due to Nebuchadnezzar's fully inhabiting his animality, letting the animal *within* him be realized in a manner that gave him experiential insight into the realm where he was once sovereign. Jonah and Daniel's representation of reality as nested—the human within the animal and the animal within the human—suggests creaturely continuity that might reorder our own relationships with the other-than-human life with whom we share a planetary home and our relationship with our own bodies and their creaturely needs and ways of knowing.

In these examples of prophetic texts in the Bible, we hear the narrators of the prophets' stories straining to imagine the recovery of right relationship with God through right relationship with the natural world. The two aspects of relationships are not distinct but rather necessarily inform each other within one holistic worldview of what is considered by the Jewish tradition as right and ethical. Living within one's limits and exercising restraint from predatory relationships to which one might have access because of one's power were the essential message of Isaiah's vision of a peaceable kin-dom. Understanding that human actions prompt creation's mourning—a motif taken up later by the apostle Paul when he speaks of creation groaning in eager expectation for release from bondage to decay (Rom 8:19–22)—instills an ethic of responsibility within the human community to make sure that all of creation flourishes and has no occasion for lamenting human systemic sinfulness characterized as broken relationships with God and others. Finally, consideration of one's place as sacred and voicing one's desire to be present—both in places recognized as sacred by habits of human worship and in natural settings—come from a very real experience of the awe and wonder that our presence in a forest, in a desert, on a mountaintop, by a riverside, or on the seashore can instill in us. In addition, consideration of oneself as animal fosters a sense of the familial relationships we can have with the rest of creation, affirming the sacred quality of all life.

GOSPELS OF CREATION: "CONSIDER THE LILIES . . ."

The Gospels are books of the Bible that open the second part of the Bible and tell in various ways about the life of Jesus, understood by Christians to be God incarnate present to the people of his time, Jewish and non-Jewish, and present in an ongoing manner for other followers of what was known at the time as simply "the Way" (Acts 9:2). Though many of Jesus's teachings involve asking the Jews of Jesus's time to reexamine their covenants and deepen their understanding of keeping them, many of his teachings are also offered in the form of stories that demonstrate Jesus's attention to the natural world. Like many of his family members and neighbors, Jesus would have had an intimate understanding of weather systems and when it was the best time to fish or to sow and harvest grain. Some of this understanding may be lost in our modern culture when food is so easily procured in supermarkets, but Jesus's intimacy with the natural cycles of the living world in which we still live is important to understanding why he used certain images in his storytelling.

One of Jesus's teachings from his so-called "Sermon on the Mount" is a favorite of contemporary readers who regularly experience their lives as distracted, anxious, and onerous. In this teaching, Jesus famously advises his followers to "consider the lilies . . ." (Matt 6:28), of which the American poet Emily Dickinson wrote, "Were all its advice so enchanting as that, we should probably heed it."[11] What Jesus's instruction seems to have meant is that his listeners were to pay attention to how parts of the natural world, including

not only flowers like the lily but birds, too, respond to their environment and are provided with what they need to survive (Matt 6:26).
Jesus basically asked his followers why they think their lives are any
different from those of other parts of creation, why they worry over
such things as whether they will have enough food to eat, clothes
to wear, and by implication, all the other needs humans have. Of
course, systemic injustice has created occasions when people have to
think about these things, some more than others, and Jesus seems
then to issue an invitation to reorder our human systems so that we
are able to live in a way that more closely resembles that of other
parts of creation that simply are, receiving what they need as they
need it, and thriving.

At one point in this passage from the Sermon on the Mount, Jesus
seems to say that human life is worth more than the birds or flowers
he has used for examples in his teaching, and when I read this com-
parison couched in the form of a question ("Are you not of more
value than they?" [Matt 6:26]), I admit to feeling troubled: Could
Jesus, an exemplary human who recognized the value of all life, have
really thought or said something like this? Does this not counter the
principles of intrinsic value and purpose? Isn't it better to read this
seemingly rhetorical question as an insertion from the anthropocentric evangelist as to what he (likely a he) thought he heard or what
he thought Jesus meant by reprimanding his disciples' anxiety in this
way? The essence of the passage is to remind the human community
of the exquisite care offered to animals and plants that is unconditionally offered by virtue of their membership in the Earth community.
And to remind human readers that they are not so different: Jesus is
calling his human listeners to attend to the fact that they too are cared
for fundamentally, apart from any "striv[ing]" (Matt 6:32), so that
they might secure their own sustenance and flourishing. We are valued unconditionally, and because of this, we too might value others
unconditionally—following divine example.

Two poets (not biblical scholars) have approached the task of identification with other-than-human agents in the biblical text to retrieve
a meaning beyond that which might have been meant or assumed

by the biblical text's original creators and later interpreters. The first poem, "What the Fig Tree Said," is by Denise Levertov.[12] In this poem, Levertov gives voice to a fig tree, which, in another troubling passage for ecologically conscious readers of the Bible, Jesus curses for not bearing fruit, even though it was not the season for figs (Mark 11:12–14). To avoid considering Jesus as a person with a temper who might express anger against the natural world for not having supplied his needs—what seems, in this passage, the unavoidably anthropocentric conclusion—biblical scholars usually point out how the fruit tree symbolized the Jewish people and how a continuity of identity is expressed between the tree not bearing fruit and the Jewish people not bearing the fruit of their ethical covenant with God, others, and the land. Levertov's poem plays with the tree's understanding of and sympathy for Jesus's action and gives voice to the fig tree's assent to having been used instrumentally in this teaching moment between Jesus, his disciples, and the reader. The tree significantly says that neither the tree nor the disciples per se were cursed, but their failures were cursed: a situation that Jesus does not want to see happen again. In part, the real failure of imagination might be ours—which balks at any personification of the natural world in this way and at the relationship between Jesus and a tree that goes beyond our understanding—a failure of imagination which Levertov's poem might heal.

Another poem by the Protestant poet Mary Oliver gives voice to the donkey who accompanied Jesus on his final procession through town before dying a gruesome death via crucifixion. Rather than using the first person pronoun to indicate voice, Oliver retains her poetic persona in this poem—announced even in the poem's title, "The Poet Thinks about the Donkey"—that considers the experience of the donkey during this episode and expresses her wish that the donkey would have experienced the event in a particular way and been celebrated for having been present for an important event in human history.[13] Yet understanding that the donkey had a life quite apart from the donkey's presence in this story about Jesus is a part of the expanded consciousness that Mary Oliver, like Levertov, asks us to practice. Through this strategy of identification, these poets undertake an important task of engaging empathetically, identifying with other figures in the biblical text besides the centralized, human characters.

Both poems suggest important vehicles for consideration of experience beyond our anthropocentric perspective. I wonder what questions or observations remain for you as you consider these poems and the perspectives they offer. Do you still hear traces of anthropocentric concern? Do you sense a shift in perspective, and what do you think could have motivated that shift? Does it matter that both poets are women? Though it is true we are incapable of saying definitively whether our views coincide with those of either a fig tree or a donkey, when we engage their experience imaginatively and empathetically, in these cases, we can use the exercise of identification to approach a wider appreciation of the diverse versions of stories that occur and perspectives that give rise to differing versions of events. By cultivating a habit of such identification, we may in fact ripen our own human identity as creatures who seem peculiarly able to imagine and empathize and may use these abilities to restore ourselves to a position of mutually enhancing relations with the rest of creation.

CONCLUSION

The Bible offers conflicting worldviews of promoting human exceptionalism while also counteracting that promotion with other images of communion. The multivoiced text of the Bible allows us to listen closely to diverse experiences of the sacred, mediated through human knowledge and limits to that knowledge, in relationship with animal others and the land. Though typically regarding themselves as made in the image of God and being given authority to dominate other parts of creation, some people are exploring images of God in new ways that correspond to new scientific knowledge. God is the life force, the originating impetus of all creation, and the power by which all that is continues. Relating with the sacred aspect of that ongoing sacred presence means uncovering the significance of our relationships with all that helps us exist and expressing our gratitude, praise, and care for all that helps us continue to exist. The Bible can be read with caution when seeming to promote oppressive relationships—between humans and between humans and animals or the land—and can be read with appreciation when seeming to promote strategies of healing broken relationships. The creation stories, prophetic passages of poetry and stories, and gospel teachings are important preliminary places to engage biblical values for ecospirituality.

Questions for Reflection and Discussion

- What are your favorite Bible stories? What more-than-human characters appear in them? What animals and plants appear in other sacred stories? What is their role or meaning?
- Is the Bible an appropriate source for environmental ethics in our time? Why or why not? What other sacred texts contain "seeds" useful for developing an environmental ethic?
- Which of the principles of intrinsic value, purpose, interconnectedness, mutual custodianship, voice, or resistance means the most to you? Why?
- How do you understand human identity and the role of humans in the Earth community? What gifts can you imagine might be part of human life that are yet unimagined?
- When have you taken time to "consider the lily" or do something similar? What insights arose for you about the nature of human life or life more generally?

Suggested Ecospiritual Practices

Write a poem that imagines the experience of a creature in a sacred story. Or write a poem that celebrates or laments some aspect of the Earth community known to you. Identify significant features of your particular bioregion or watershed and experiment with voice to express what you imaginatively intuit the trees, mountains, lakes, or animals in your bioregion might be saying were we able to hear their voices speaking our own languages. Try to listen for resistant voices too: What might creation say in resistance to human activities of domination or exploitation? Whether your poem voices lament or celebration, find an outdoor space in which you can proclaim aloud (or even sing) your poem and experience a time of communion with your neighbors in nature. Consider this an invitation to compose your own articulation that gives voice to life, a sacred endeavor becoming sacred text.

Practice accessing your own inner animality. If you live with companion animals, be present with them in a way that celebrates your commonality: You both eat, sleep, stretch, and yawn. At times, you both play. Perhaps you climb trees or run for the pleasure of running or to chase something. You might swim and immerse yourself in the world of the ocean and sea creatures. What are some other ways that you notice your body coming alive in the presence of animals or as a feature of your self-understanding as a particular kind of animal, capable of imagination and self-reflection? It has been said that "animals make us human." In what way do you understand or experience the truth of that claim? Do animals make us human in the sense of drawing a sharp contrast between us as living beings? Or do animals make us human in the sense of calling forth our deepest identities of caregiving and affection in ways animals themselves might model for us? Consider this an invitation to deepen your experience of being a person in creaturely continuity with many other living creatures in our world.

For Further Reading

Eco Bible, Volume 1: An Ecological Commentary on Genesis and Exodus by Rabbi Yonatan Neril and Rabbi Leo Dee (Interfaith Center for Sustainable Development, 2020)

The Hebrew Bible and Environmental Ethics: Humans, Nonhumans, and the Living Landscape by Mari Joerstad (Cambridge University Press, 2019)

An Inconvenient Text: Is a Green Reading of the Bible Possible? by Norman C. Habel (ATF, 2009)

The Splendor of Creation: A Biblical Ecology by Ellen Bernstein (Pilgrim, 2005)

Unsettling the Word: Biblical Experiments in Decolonization edited by Steve Heinrichs (Orbis, 2019)

CHAPTER TWO
The Christian Desert Tradition

> The external deserts in the world are growing, because the internal deserts have become so vast.
>
> —Pope Benedict XVI,
> quoted in Pope Francis's *Laudato si'*

Early followers of Jesus's way saw his life as portrayed in the Gospels as a template for their own faith expressions. This involved not only acts of social engagement, such as preaching and baptizing as the "Great Commission" instructed (Matt 28:16–20), but also acts of healing and sharing. These latter examples of Christian life appear in the book of Acts when early faith communities were figuring out how they might best embody the principles Jesus lived by, such as belonging, sharing, and forgiveness. There was quite a bit of diversity among his followers, and by the fourth century, the so-called desert Christians were embodying their understanding of a Christ-life through imitation of Jesus's act of retreating into the wilderness to pray (Mark 3:7, for example). It was thought that this action would enable Christians to wean themselves from distractions caused by the social world of the marketplace, family, and church politics; allow them to focus on their relationship with God; and eventually, make them more authentically available to one another, having dealt with some of their own most troubling inclinations and temptations.

Eventually, this action of retreat to Egyptian, Syrian, and Palestinian deserts became paradigmatic of an entire way of relating to God by immersion into the natural world, saturated with the sacred indwelling of divine presence. Even today, many monastic communities, or places where people who have dedicated themselves to a particular expression of religious life live in community, are set in natural environments that invite repose of body and soul and deliberately distance community members and visitors from other people and their activities. Though many of the desert Christians lived alone in natural dwellings made of sunbaked clay or carved out of rock, they also visited one another regularly, soliciting practical advice about securing food, water, and materials for their handcrafts. They also sought other practical advice such as the following: How might one get through a day that could become long once minimal needs for survival had been met? How did one deal with temptations to not only survive but thrive materially by accruing wealth and status? If God were not discerned as present all the time, how might one resist the urge to just give it all up and go back to town? How might one deal with loneliness and the longing for company and love that might be only temporarily assuaged by a person's visit? Those who toughed it out in these settings, off the grid both literally and ecclesiastically, found themselves eventually transforming into people who were more gracious as guests with one another, with the wild creatures with whom they shared their desert wilderness home, and even with themselves. These women and men acquired a reputation as hardy figures who masochistically went without things just to prove their dedication to God. But in fact, many found themselves transformed beyond their wildest dreams by spending a significant time alone in the desert, an experience many wilderness backpackers have shared.

Though these desert Christians may have inherited some disturbing ideas about the material world as evil (some of them even thought their own bodies were evil) and in need of redemptive care (or self-discipline, often severe), they also transformed their dominating tendencies toward the natural world into attitudes of loving care and interconnectedness. In fact, an almost fable-like kind of harmony arose around these figures who could relate favorably with animals—even those animals typically hostile to human presence, such as snakes and crocodiles—and with the elements of the natural world, especially settings typically inhospitable to human presence. These are traits that seeded the lives and work of medieval men and women in Christian faith communities and continue to seed our own spiritual ways of life today.

LOVE FOR A HOME IN THE WILD
AND DELIGHT IN OTHER CREATURES

One of the most famous of the desert Christians was a man named Antony who lived in Egypt from 251 to 356 CE. When he was a young man, Antony's parents died, and he went to church and felt God was calling him to a life that would require that he give up his social position and his family's land.[1] Following this call, Antony left everything to visit the elders who lived around his hometown. Perhaps he was looking for some surrogate parent to take the place of his mother and father. He did begin to form relationships with these elders and eventually moved farther into the desert, where he could be pretty much all by himself. There, he was visited periodically by friends who brought him bread. Over time, these friends could see that significant periods of solitude were transforming Antony into a more joyful and serene person. In fact, if you do the math in calculating his age, you'll see that Antony lived to be 105 years old. His friend and biographer, a Christian bishop of Alexandria named Athanasius, even tells us that at the end of Antony's life, "he possessed eyes undimmed and sound, and he saw clearly. He lost none of his teeth— they simply had been worn to the gums because of the old man's great age. He also retained health in his feet and hands, and generally he seemed brighter and of more energetic strength than those who make use of baths and a variety of foods and clothing."[2] Clearly, something about Antony's life choices worked for him!

Antony's first years in the desert, however, were characterized by intense struggle. Athanasius tells us that Antony had to fight his expectations of peace of mind, which, given their cultural milieu, they referred to as facing demons. Whether those demons were real

or imagined really makes no difference considering the grave combat into which the solitary person was thought to enter when setting themselves apart from others. This self-isolating tendency can
be problematic when a whole tradition grows up around valoriz-
ing loneliness and the sacrifice of things (especially essential things
like sleep and food) and relationships that are legitimately helpful
in one's spiritual growth. On the other hand, the desert Christians
remind us of the value of the Earth community's providing a context in which we meaningfully encounter our deepest selves and
that which is sacred. We all need some amount of time on our own
and in the proverbial desert—whether that be just looking at the
stars in one's backyard in the quiet of a dark night or walking on
the seashore or retreating to a city park for a slow walk among the
trees. The more we normalize such experiences and integrate them
into our daily lives wherever we are, the better off we and the whole
Earth community will be.

Eventually Antony's idyllic way of life drew attention, and others
wanted to visit him, enjoy the natural setting in which he was living out his Christian life, and learn from him how they too might
live such a blessed life. It was at this point that Antony moved even
farther into the wilderness and found what he called the "Inner
Mountain." There, the stories about him tell us, he found a place
he loved. Athanasius describes this place: "Below the hill there was
water—perfectly clear, sweet and quite cold, and beyond there were
plains, and a few untended date palms. Then Antony, as if stirred by
God, fell in love with the place. . . . Looking on it as his own home,
from that point forward he stayed in that place. . . . [He] inspected
the land around the mountain, and finding a small, suitable place he
plowed it; and having abundant water from the spring, he planted
it. . . . [He] loved more than everything else his way of life in the
mountain."[3] Having found a place to call home, Antony was able
to construct a dwelling for himself, plant a small garden, and enjoy
the fruits of the palm trees growing nearby. Though he continued to
be visited by pilgrims who wanted to see such a famous old man
living alone, he grew increasingly tolerant of and even came to enjoy

their presence, and he taught them from his own experience. There are *sayings*, or spiritual teachings, from and about him and others like him that continue to influence people who live the monastic lifestyle within Christianity and even those within other traditions. Many have remarked on the resonance between the gnomic wisdom of the Christian desert sayings and Zen Buddhist wisdom for their sparse, poetic attention to what seems to really matter. Some of the habits of being that were developed among the desert Christians that resonate with the fruit of Buddhist practice include a quality of inner peace, attention to one's real rather than imagined needs, prayer and meditation, and even bodily practices like mindful eating.

The charm of Antony's story is his love for his home and way of life in the wild. The charm of another desert Christian's story is his delight in other creatures. This story is about a desert Christian named Theon and conveys a lot of what seems to have impressed pilgrims who visited the desert Christians. Theon was exceptional as a miracle-worker and clairvoyant, and he healed many of his ailing visitors. The storytellers said of him, "One could see him with the face of an angel giving joy to his visitors by his gaze and abounding with much grace."[4] But it was really his relationship with his home in the desert and with other creatures of the wild that most captured something important about the companionability made possible by his coming to see through and dismantle his anthropocentric tendency to dominate or subdue other creatures to his will. The storytellers told, "He ate vegetables but only those that did not need to be cooked. They say that he used to go out of his cell at night and keep company with wild animals, giving them to drink from the water which he had. Certainly, one could see the tracks of antelope and wild asses and gazelle and other animals near his hermitage. *These creatures delighted him always.*"[5] Theon ate only vegetables—as was imagined was the case in the garden of Eden—recapturing something of that primeval harmony described in the biblical creation stories. He ate them uncooked, significantly, meaning that he did not use parts of creation as fuel to make the food possibly more palatable but made do with what was available. Unlike others who might have been bothered by the wild animals or who might have hunted the animals for sport or food, Theon's experience of those with whom he shared a wilderness home was one of delight. This helps us remember that our own engagement with those with whom we share our homes might also be characterized by delight. Antony and Theon likely would not have become the joyful and peaceful men they became—nor lovers of their desert homes capable of delighting in their other-than-human neighbors—if they had remained at home in cities, busily trying to earn a living there by buying and selling as would otherwise have been necessary.

For those of us who live in cities, this reality may seem disheartening and may reinforce the relocation suggested by the metaphor of spiritual journey that I earlier critiqued. We are offered the opportunity in our everyday encounters with the wildlife in our cities to be mindful that the city/rural divide is not quite as large as we imagine. As Syncletica, another desert Christian, taught, "There are many who live in the mountains and behave as if they were in the town, and they are wasting their time. It is possible to be a solitary in one's mind while living in a crowd, and it is possible for one who is solitary to live in the crowd of [one's] own thoughts."[6] Syncletica reminds us that there are certain attitudes activated by our surroundings—certain ways of being that are natural to the wilderness setting and can be transgressed if a person is distracted by other things. She also reminds us that even within a crowd, we can be mindful of others and our own internal and outer landscapes, even letting these provoke delight within us rather than consternation. Our attitude toward the place where we are determines how conducive that place is to allowing and assisting us to awaken to the sacred that is always present.

DESERT WISDOM AS GOING OUTSIDE AND STAYING WITHIN

John Muir, an enthusiastic hiker, advocate for the National Park system in the United States, and founder of the Sierra Club, famously wrote, "I only went out for a walk, and finally concluded to stay out till sundown, for going out, I found, was really going in."[7] This might have described a single day's experience for Muir or an entire lifetime devoted to experiencing the woods, deserts, and mountains of the United States. Whenever he seems to have gone out, literally and figuratively, he found himself going further in. To what? Mystery? His deepest identity as one akin to all the rest of creation? It is hard to know, given the paradoxical nature of what he tried to describe. The desert Christians, too, lived the paradoxical experience of going farther into the wilderness and further into their own deepest identities when rooted in these unfamiliar places.

The wisdom of these desert Christians is drawn from their experience of the difficulty of living alone and in the wild, far from company and resources readily available elsewhere. Yet this very place of seeming deprivation might also be a source of replenishment and joy. Antony, for instance, taught, "When you are moved by thoughts that distress you and that you cannot chase away sufficiently, go outside into the fresh air and they will leave you."[8] This advice might apply to his entire life. Distressed by the death of his parents and the responsibilities of land ownership and caring for his sibling, Antony went outside by moving to the desert. But in the daily rhythm as well, going outdoors provides relief from the stressors that accompany anyone's life, whether that person lives in a remote desert or an urban setting. Fresh air restores. Sunlight restores. Green grass and trees, blossoms and fallen leaves restore. The scurrying or flying of other creatures restores.

On the other hand, Antony also taught his friends and visitors to stay put as opposed to "going out." In particular, he presented staying in one's dwelling as a remedy for various temptations that distract oneself from the real things of life—like one's occasional boredom, weariness, anger, and other things that he seems to have thought worth engaging, despite or even because of the tension they might produce—for optimal spiritual growth. He taught, "Just as fish die if they are on dry land for some time, so do monks [those devoted to a solitary life] who loiter outside their cells [or dwellings] or waste time . . . release themselves from the tension of *hesychia* [inner still-ness]. So we should hasten back to the cell (like the fish to the sea) lest while loitering outside we forget to keep a watch on the inner self."⁹ In this teaching, Antony reminds others, and likely himself too, about their proper place in creation. Though many subsequent monastic readers might have taken this particular teaching to mean they ought to remain in their monastery homes all the time, contemporary read-ers might interpret this teaching as revealing that there are proper dwellings for humans to inhabit, just as fish inhabit the sea. Further-more, such an interpretation might point out that it is deadly for humans to go beyond places appropriate for their habitation—deadly for themselves and potentially for others. Again, the monastic archi-vists of this literature would have liked this saying to mean that they ought to stay in their literal homes and not venture into the towns or cities where others lived, solidifying a distinction between sacred and secular space that might appear suspect to us today. Yet Antony's vision should be seen as expanding beyond the strictures that would come to be associated with Christian and other traditions' monastic lives. His attention was on resisting the fatal attraction of bioregions not conducive to human life. As we encroach on the wilderness habi-tats of many other creatures' lives, we do a fatal injustice to them and to ourselves. Rather, our experience should be one of radical hospitality within our earthly home that prevents our depriving others of their homes while allowing us to welcome others with whom we live into the spaces we can harmoniously coinhabit. This requires compassion-ate discernment if we experience ourselves as increasingly alienated from our earthly home in ways that attract us beyond the borders of human habitation, into wilderness areas better left in peace and per-haps only visited in moderation and with great respect for the others who live there.

This desert saying and many others like it demonstrate an under-standing of the continuity between humans and other life-forms, like fish and other creatures. When Antony says, "Just as . . ." about a fish's life to speak about human life, his listeners and we understand him. Another saying speaks of a desert Christian who seems to have taken Antony's teaching to heart and taken refuge in his desert dwelling when others came to visit him. When asked why he did this, he replied, "The wild animals who take refuge in their dens are saved."[10] This answer implies that the visitors were metaphorical hunters and that it was necessary for this desert Christian to avoid destruction of himself when engaging the other by removing himself from the danger. Naturally, this kind of saying does damage in a tradition that fosters thinking about social interactions as disruptions to one's own spiritual development, but it can also help us think about the many profound spiritual teachings that come from the natural world and how animals model behavior for us to follow. Another desert Christian affirmed, perhaps as many modern people who live with dogs could, "A dog is better than me, for a dog has love and does not go passing judgment."[11] If reminded of these realities of kinship and creaturely continuity as the desert Christians offer them to us, we may pay more attention to the natural world. Just as wild animals take refuge in their dens, so might humans also find places of refuge appropriate to themselves. Further, just as humans might refrain from being the reason wild animals seek refuge, so we might treat each other in ways that do not initiate retreat. The principle of mutual custodianship requires that we do better for one another, human and animal, than creating occasions for fear and fleeing. We might also take lessons from the animals who daily accompany us with love and reciprocate that acceptance with others.

WOMEN AND WILDERNESS

Numerous writers today align the wilderness of the natural world with the interior landscapes of our human identity, suggesting an important continuity between the inner and outer that we might too often try to keep separated. For instance, in Pope Francis's 2015 encyclical on creation care, we are told, "The external deserts in the world are growing, because the internal deserts have become so vast."[12] This means that our lives have become so dry and barren as a result of consumerism and addiction that we end up imposing such a dryness and barrenness on the rest of creation as we build farther into habitats that should not be impacted by our human presence, just in order to try to satisfy our inner thirsts in ways that are ultimately not satisfying. One of the first visuals of this that comes to mind is a place from my youth and my coastal hometown where a mall—the city's first—was built right along the seashore, encroaching on the coastal landscape and the countless creatures who made their home there. It was great fun for me as a young person to have a mall in our town where I got my ears pierced and saw movies and ate pizza and bought my own clothing and could hang out with friends, but certainly, the goods and experiences available in that space were purchased at a price and pursued at a price, satisfying thirsts that presence in the natural world could satisfy. This desertification, internal and external, that Pope Francis's encyclical describes is something we are invited to step beyond, even as we affirm the value of places that are desert. Other modern writers, such as David Abram, Paul Wapner, Marc Bekoff, and Bill Plotkin, also engage wilderness as a vital means by which humans might recover experience of their own interior wilderness.[13] The hopeful thesis these authors pursue is that as we reconnect with those places within, we will lessen our destructive impacts on our exterior home.

Many, many individuals long to retreat to the wilderness to get away from the stress of modern society, and the desert Christians are perceived as having been motivated by this longing too. Not only was the crumbling of the Roman Empire imminent and an expectation of Jesus's return shaping the consciousness of Christians in the fourth century—mirroring, in a sense, our own sense of ecoapocalypse in a time of climate change, global warming, and species extinctions—but the desert Christians also lived in a time when the Christian church was growing in authority. Christians were gaining power and prestige in the Roman Empire, and those who were wealthy and secure socially and financially often adopted Christianity as a political expedient, putting them in favor with the emperor and others with power. This led to an uncertainty about what it meant to be a practicing Christian—could one in fact live in an opulent dwelling, have slaves, eat and drink more than one needed, and still be a Christian? Many people read the Gospels and found Jesus's model of a simpler life more consistent with what they felt themselves called to live—a life more socially just and more ecologically friendly and one lived apart from activities characterized by lack of compassion. Similarly, as our lives become increasingly urban and interiorly focused in our homes or jobs or technologies, something of our spirit yearns for the sacred presence felt in the outdoors. Men like Henry David Thoreau and John Muir sought to defend the wilderness against human exploitation, and both of these men enjoyed significant amounts of time alone in the wilderness. More recently, Chris McCandless, a young man exploring in the Alaskan wilderness, died tragically and alone.[14] Sometimes, these forays into wilderness are dangerous, both physically and emotionally. Yet that they continue to occur suggests something essential about what they provide the human spirit.

You may note that so far in this chapter, save for the mention of Syncletica, I have only referred to men. The theme of "escape into the wilderness" *has* largely been a masculine ideal in many cultures because domestic roles typically ascribed to the female have kept women close to the home and the tasks of housekeeping and child-rearing that occur there. Yet there were desert Christians who were female whose encounters with the sacred earth were profound and led to their assuming an authority, often exercised in different ways than that exercised by men, over the pilgrims who came to visit them. However, there were not many of them whose stories and teachings were remembered or saved for future readers. In fact, it is worth noting that many of these women had to make more difficult and risky decisions than men to forego life experiences like marriage and creating families and have the kind of life made possible by desert solitude, due to the social norms of their times.

More recently, the domination of exploration of wilderness terrain by men has come into feminist critique in contemporary literature as women experience their own time alone in the desert as restorative of something fundamentally human that they historically have, as wives and mothers, often seemed to be deprived of. Cheryl Strayed's *Wild*, which documents Strayed's experience on the Pacific Coast Trail, is one example of a woman's story that interrupts the dominance of men in wilderness tales of survival and transformation.[15] Similarly, Abi Andrews' *The Word for Woman Is Wilderness* documents one young woman's resistance to the dominance in the American cultural narrative of men's experiences of the wild and to the kind of toxic masculinity that can emerge from that dominance.[16] Andrews does not accept the premise that women are not as strong as men or not as drawn to experience the natural world. Her novel's protagonist undertakes an arduous pilgrimage to the site of Chris McCandless' Alaskan hermitage to explore on-site her critical engagement with men's dominance of wilderness spaces. While doing this, she reflects on the social pressures on men and women that make the escape to wilderness felt to be necessary. By implication, her work calls us to reexamine these values.

The wilderness is, in fact, becoming an equal opportunity place in terms of gender. However, women, proponents of feminist care ethics, and disability scholars are calling out ecoableist tendencies in our conversations about the experience of being outdoors and our promotion of some forms of eco-friendly activities over others. In terms of access, however, not everyone has the financial means or the physical ability to retreat too far into the wilderness, especially alone—historically, women have been among those not having access. Idealizing the wilderness experience of a person whose strength is tested by the loneliness and the physical demands of being in the wild can in fact be a dangerous cultural construction in our time and can be ecoableist—the privileging of outdoor activities and eco-friendly practices that able-bodied persons can engage easily. Ecoableism discounts the contributions that persons without ready access to wilderness can make to our understanding of the significance and meaning of wilderness for all of us. Ecospirituality must have flexible borders when we consider whose experience of the sacred within the context of the natural world counts. We might ask, whose records remain of these experiences and when and how they get foregrounded in our cultural discourse of environmental change and the promotion of healthy relationships within our Earth community?

Furthermore, extreme sports and reality television—often, though not always, dominated by masculine and able-bodied individuals—tend to glorify survival skills that often put a burden on wilderness sites where animals make a home, not to mention the burden on those animals themselves when their presence becomes known. In addition, the testing of one's skill, will, and discipline in the context of combat with a wilderness setting is extremely dangerous psychologically. There are helpful ways to learn to use one's ability to be present in nature to heal psychological wounds in ways that do not harm others. We need to replace war-like metaphors when engaging with things that are difficult or inhospitable with seeing ourselves more at home and belonging within the natural world. We need to apply some rules of courtesy that we apply in our own homes to our forays into wilderness where we may be equally at home and yet also at the same time a guest. The more we green our cities and are nourished by our everyday encounters with the wildlife with whom we share our neighborhoods, the less we will hunger for the solitary experience of being alone in the wild.

CONTEMPORARY COMMITMENTS

The desert Christian tradition led to the development of Benedictine monasticism and subsequent religious orders in the Christian churches that are Orthodox, Catholic, and even Protestant. Though much of the literary wealth and wisdom of this premonastic period is still available to nonmonastic specialists, the rest of the contemporary Christian community hardly knows of this period or its insightful literature characterized by withdrawal to and celebration of the natural world. Ecological renewals, however, are emerging rapidly from contemporary Christian monastic communities, so it behooves Christian faith communities and others to look to these ancient models still existing among us for how to live more harmoniously with our natural environments.

Sarah McFarland Taylor's work with women whom she calls "green sisters" in the Catholic faith community is fascinating in terms of how it showcases the work of women of faith having made commitments to green their monastic commitments. For instance, traditional monastic vows of obedience, chastity, and poverty are rehabilitated by these green sisters to indicate a way of life open to many. The vow of obedience becomes a commitment to "learning how live 'within one's niche' and within the bounds of the local ecological resources without encroaching on the habitats of others"; the vow of chastity becomes "a moral commitment to ease ecosystem stresses," not limited to population growth, and to exercise restraint from that which anesthetizes a person, such as "noise . . . over-eating and drinking, TV, acquiring, over-working"; and the vow of poverty becomes a commitment to voluntary simplicity.[17] Furthermore, these women impressively model an attitude of calling into question the distinction between spiritual and ecological practices. Taylor notes the nitty-gritty decisions that these sisters routinely make regarding choice of clothing, food, transportation, recreation, and even building materials for their communal homes that constitute not merely material choices but spiritual choices. One green sister explains,

> To practice the discipline of discerning what's "enough" at any one moment . . . the discipline of purchasing products out of a growing ecological sensitivity and responsibly dealing with discarded paper, metal, glass plastic . . . the discipline of reducing the use of a car . . . the discipline of choosing and using eco-sensitive washing products . . . the discipline of reducing electricity and moderating one's use of fossil fuels . . . ALL OF THIS AFFECTS MY SPIRIT . . . and therefore is a practice of my SPIRIT. Are they "practical disciplines"? Yes. Are they "spiritual practices"? Yes . . . It's all connected to my Spirit dimension. We cannot be separated out—body from Spirit, mind from body, mind from Spirit . . . practical from spiritual . . . consumer products from prayer . . . it's all of a piece for me. So everything becomes a "spiritual dimension" in all my choices. Consumer choices are integral to this. Dichotomies are not helpful to me.[18]

These words resonate with Terry Tempest Williams's words on the interrelatedness between soul and soil. This particular excerpt from Taylor's book, which is built of ethnographic evidence she gathered from different Catholic communities, resonates with many other descriptions of women's concrete choices that are integrative of their physical, social, and spiritual lives. While many men's communities are also innovating in important ways, women's practices of ethical care for animals, plants, and places have readily evolved with their devotional commitments in their communities in a manner quite distinct from those of men. Taylor's *Green Sisters* is a fascinating resource for those outside monastic communities, as well as for those within such communities, for consideration of how the practical and spiritual are entangled in our everyday lives.

Women are also innovating within the field of ecosexuality, which characterizes the relationship one has toward Earth as love. Though anthropomorphism of Earth often takes a female form (the Gaia hypothesis draws on ancient, mythic representations of Earth as a goddess) and more specifically a maternal form (Mother Earth or Mother Nature), ecosexuals—many of whom identify as women—regard this metaphor as insufficient, and they urge movement in our thinking and in our actions toward regarding Earth as lover and beloved. Ecosexuality is defined as a "cultural practice that enables our species to reconnect our metabolism with the metabolism of the Earth. A movement of movements in which a broad range of interrelated social, environmental, cultural, and economic efforts converge around the shared vision of sustainable, fluid, inclusive practices of love that bring people together around love for the partner we all share: the Earth."[19] Further, ecosexual thought describes the relationship between care for the ecosystem that is a larger aspect of the home (or lover) we all share and the care we show for the ecosystems we *are*. Each of us is made up of countless living organisms. Ecosexuality "offers a living laboratory in which theory, practice, activism, and creativity can converge and generate community around the interconnected elements of sex, love, intimacy, sustainability, artistic expression, open relating, and land-based living."[20]

Those identifying as ecosexuals often stage theatrical marriages that involve commitments to a human partner and also some aspect of the natural world the couple is committed to preserving and caring for. The Ecosex Manifesto ends with the pledge, "I promise to love, honor and cherish you Earth, until death brings us closer together forever."[21] This pledge of course plays with the terminology sometimes used between human lovers as they marry and express commitment to one another until death parts them. In the Ecosex Manifesto, the recognition is made that, in fact, at death we will draw closer together substantially as every aspect of our material being comes into contact with the rest of the Earth community.

Like the green sisters and ecosexual movement, another development of commitment and communal life that is ecumenical and interreligious and draws from the monastic tradition and the love that Antony felt toward his wild home and Theon toward his animal neighbors is the Order of the Sacred Earth. This new interfaith order was created by Matthew Fox and his friends as a pan-generational expression of how people might use the structure of the historical pattern of monastic life—the "order"—without many of its restrictive dimensions. For instance, rather than make vows of celibacy, obedience, and poverty as many other Christian monastics do, members of the Order of the Sacred Earth offer one simple vow: *I promise to be the best lover and defender of the Earth that I can be.*[22] Small pods of members of this order meet regularly to help each other ritualize and keep this commitment. While the "defender" imagery in this vow may evoke troubling conflict-ridden and warrior-centered associations, this vow brings a celebratory feeling for the Earth community alongside courageous action in solidarity with vulnerable members of the Earth community. This vow reminds us of our power and privilege as human members of the Earth community, and the vow expresses resolve to use that power and privilege wisely and on behalf of others with less power.

CONCLUSION

The desert Christians often experienced loneliness where they were living off the grid. They had a word for their experience: *acedia*. This is not a word we often use or recognize now, but it describes an experience quite familiar to many: listlessness, depression, weariness, uneasiness. The desert Christians who wrote of this experience said it happened when they reached the true silence of the desert and their own noisiness had not yet ceased. Rather than rest in the compassionate presence of God or the sacred presence, these desert Christians felt anxious. They wanted to be doing something; they wanted to be making a difference. They had been habituated or socialized to think of themselves as worthy or valuable only because of what they produced. To encounter the gifts of the natural world as undeserved, even as indicating unconditional love, felt uncomfortable, just as it might feel uncomfortable for us to be unable to repay the earth for the abundance we enjoy, to be utterly beholden to some dimension quite beyond ourselves. The loneliness of the desert Christians is mirrored also in contemporary experiences of *biophobia* or nature-deficit disorder, when human beings experience uneasiness in the natural world, and *species loneliness*, when human beings experience feeling cut off from the rest of creation.[23] Ecospirituality invites us to consider how to alleviate our creaturely loneliness with respectful companionship with one another and with the others with whom we share a home. Being present in deliberate ways, letting our relationships of love and care develop as we spend time attentive and responsive to the natural world, is the foundation of ecospiritual practice.

Questions for Reflection and Discussion

- Which animals or plants do you feel an affinity or even love for? What do they teach you about possibilities for experiencing and understanding your own life?
- When have you been able to be alone in nature? What was it like? How is your experience of the natural world different when you are accompanied by other humans?
- How do you experience a city's greenspace? Where have you met wildlife in the city and how do you live companionably with wildlife wherever you live?
- How might you better love and defend the earth? Do these seem like worthwhile commitments to you? Why or why not?
- What kind of vow for eco-action might you be drawn to make? How might you formalize that vow, remain mindful of it, and share it with others?

Suggested Ecospiritual Practices

Lectio divina is a practice of reading meditatively that springs from early Christian devotional life and involves the four steps of reading, meditating, praying, and contemplating. As a person reads words that invite transformation, that person slows down to consider what the words are calling them to in terms of a response or resolution. I invite you to read the desert saying below slowly and carefully as you consider the "seeds" that are sown in your life that may be in danger of being trampled by you accidentally. What might begin to show itself when you rest and are quiet enough in body and mind, emotions and spirit, to sense it? After you are done reading, reflecting on what calls to you, and responding or resolving, spend some time resting. Monastic writers in the Christian tradition used language of *rumination* to align their own meditative, prayerful reading with the work of ruminants, cows or camels, who chew cud, meaning their process of digestion is delayed and slow. So might our consumption of material offer us spiritual growth. Monastic writers thought of themselves as able to glean important nourishment from sacred words as they slowed down to mull over and respond to what the words invited. Consider imitating this practice as you read the following: "In the same way that no plant whatsoever grows up on a well-trodden highway, not even if you sow seed, because the surface is trodden down, so it is with us. Withdraw from all business into [inner stillness] and you will see things growing that you did not know were in you, for you were walking on them."[24] You might also practice *lectio mundi*, or meditative reading of the natural world. How might you sit with a plant and consider the plant's fragility and resiliency as modeling how you might also grow and be? How might you be present with an animal and consider the lifeway of that animal as modeling particular wisdom by which you might also grow and be? Consider this an invitation to grow your kinship with and delight in other members of the Earth community and to marvel at all we share.

For Further Reading

The Blue Sapphire of the Mind: Notes for a Contemplative Ecology by Douglas E. Christie (Oxford University Press, 2013)

Earth, Our Original Monastery: Cultivating Wonder and Gratitude through Intimacy with Nature by Christine Valters Paintner (Sorin, 2020)

Green Sisters: A Spiritual Ecology by Sarah McFarland Taylor (Harvard University Press, 2007)

The Sacred Desert: Religion, Literature, Art, and Culture by David Jasper (Blackwell, 2004)

The Solace of Fierce Landscapes: Exploring Desert and Mountain Spirituality by Belden C. Lane (Oxford University Press, 1998)

CHAPTER THREE

Saints Francis and Hildegard

I said to the almond tree, "Sister, speak to me of God."
And the almond tree blossomed.
—Nikos Kazantzakis, *Report to Greco*

Saint Francis and Saint Hildegard are two exemplars in the Christian spiritual tradition whose experiential engagements with the sacred in the natural world might be seen as "seeds" representing possibilities for others' and our own experiences. While these figures are rooted in a specific religious tradition, the principles that can be drawn from their ecospiritual experience and practice might inform and inspire any person's engagement with the natural world, regardless of that person's religious identity and commitments. Francis of Assisi, for instance, celebrated the kinship of creation in a way that can assist our own experience and understanding of relationship with more-than-human others. Hildegard of Bingen's therapeutic engagement with the natural world and her description of a green power she called *viriditas* collapse the duality between the divine and the natural world and can occasion our own recognition of the sacred earth and effect our own experiences of restoration and healing of our own identities and our relationships with the rest of creation.

Just as these figures may be seen as "seeds," so too might they be seen as icons of ecospirituality. In the Orthodox Christian tradition, icons are of particular importance as images that operate in a sacramental manner, as a portal of sorts between this and another world. In the Celtic Christian world, "thin places" also operate this way as a thinning of whatever seems to separate us from another world. Use of this imagery in this chapter is meant to help us think past the distinctions between these two and focus on the blurring of such boundaries until, in fact, they might be erased entirely. Aspects of transcendence and immanence are fundamental to religious consideration of the "location" of the divine, especially when considered as a creator who would necessarily transcend the creator's creation. However, we might also focus on and emphasize the continuity between the transcendent and immanent as a strategy for reinhabiting the sacred earth and sacred cosmos of which we all form a small albeit significant part.

Saints Francis and Hildegard certainly encountered the natural world in ways shaped by their own historical and cultural contexts, but they also challenged their contemporaries to think and to be in new ways. As we listen to their voices over the space of many centuries, we are invited to move beyond our anthropocentric bias and our assumptions about the world we live in and the identities we have and share. This stretching open of our thinking and being has the potential to enhance our well-being and the flourishing for which all creatures share a longing. Francis and Hildegard represent individuals whose radical resistance to the conventions of their own time function ably to call us out beyond our typical ways of being, thinking, and doing. Other individuals, such as the desert Christians discussed in the previous chapter, also do that. Moreover, venerated figures in other wisdom traditions, whether founders of or innovators within movements, such as the ancient Chinese poet Lao Tzu or the eighth century Sufi poet Rabia, also provide us with resources from their wisdom writings drawing from their own experiential engagement of the sacred—for Lao Tzu, the Tao, and for Rabia, the Beloved—that allow us to rethink our own experience of and ethical commitments to the world we live in today, populated by a diverse human population and even more diverse living population.

As we survey sources in various wisdom traditions, we note many seeds that have continued to grow across varying geographical locations, flourishing when they find amenable soil and the nourishment they need for growth. Surveying these sources and continuing to regard them as seeds that might grow in our own experience of and thinking about the natural world remind us that others in our own time today are also challenging traditional ways of thinking and drawing on their own innovative ways of experiencing and regarding the natural world. For example, the new knowledge that science has offered us in the past century or so and continues to offer us—about human identity, the age of our world, and the creaturely continuity we share with all that is—has opened many seemingly locked doors in our understanding and perception of the world we share. The seeds provided by Francis and Hildegard for thinking anew about our own presence in a sacred universe offer us a radical belonging within the vast Earth community and even larger cosmic universe and offer us healing as well as a result of our recovered sense of identity as belonging.

FRANCIS: A BROTHER FOR ALL CREATURES

Francis of Assisi (1182–1226) was an Italian Catholic born into a family of wealthy merchants. His life story is one of radical simplicity in challenging the economic disparity of his time and committing himself to living among the marginalized. He famously and metaphorically courted a lifestyle symbolized by a companion whom he called Lady Poverty and expressed his love for and commitment to her in ways that often made others around him uncomfortable. The founder of what would become known as the Franciscans, Francis encouraged his friends and followers to live vulnerably, dependent on the hospitality and generosity of others while recognizing God as the ultimate sacred source of provisioning—just as other creatures may be seen as relying on God's provisioning through the natural ecosystems of which they form a part. Not only a friend of the poor and sick, Francis also courted the natural world, celebrating an understanding of kinship with the natural world that is unsurpassed in Christian tradition and for which Lynn White in the classic essay critiquing Christianity for its privileged role in ecological crisis, due to anthropocentric thinking, also argued that Francis should be regarded the patron saint of ecology. White wrote that the "key to an understanding of Francis is his belief in the virtue of humility—not merely for the individual but for man [or the human] as a species. Francis tried to depose man from his monarchy over creation and set up a democracy of all God's creatures."[1] For this reason, Francis is a counterexample to Christianity's anthropocentrism, a subversive revolutionary within the tradition offering another way of being Christian and of understanding the role of the human within a larger context of living beings.

Francis was also famous for having preached to birds[2]—the reason so many sculptures of him are found in gardens or even take the form of bird baths. Equally famous, his interaction with the ferocious wolf of Gubbio is among the best stories told of Francis's life.[3] In this story of the wolf of Gubbio, Francis intercedes on behalf of villagers who had been terrorized by a wolf living in their vicinity. Not afraid and feeling compassion for the animal, Francis asked the wolf to leave the villagers alone, and a covenant was entered into between the villagers and the wolf in which the villagers pledged to provide food for the wolf and the wolf pledged to refrain from attacking the villagers' livestock. In their conversation, Francis significantly addressed this wolf of Gubbio as "Friar Wolf," friar being a form of address adopted by his human community members. Thus notably, Francis is extending his understanding of contemplative community to include members of the animal world, even those who strike its human members with terror. In short, this story that demonstrates respect and compassion, reciprocity and restraint, also displays the quintessential characteristics of Franciscan ecospirituality living on into the current century and perhaps expressed by Pope Francis, with his assuming Francis's name when becoming pope.

Another important expression of Francis's sense of kinship with creation appears in his famous Canticle of the Sun in which he names the elements of creation as his family members:

Be praised, my Lord, with all your creatures,
especially Sir Brother Sun,
who is the day and through whom You give us light.
And he is beautiful and radiant with great splendor;
and bears a likeness of You, most high One.
Praised be You, my Lord, through Sister Moon and the stars;
in heaven You formed them clear and precious and beautiful.
Praised be You, my Lord, through Brother Wind,
and through the air, cloudy and serene, and every kind of weather
through which You give sustenance to Your creatures.
Praised be You, my Lord, through Sister Water,
who is very useful and humble and precious and chaste.
Praised be You, my Lord, through Brother Fire,
through whom You light the night,
and he is beautiful and playful and robust and strong.
Praised be You, my Lord, through our Sister Mother Earth,
who sustains and governs us,
and who produces varied fruits with colored flowers and herbs.[4]

This canticle is an important document in Christian spiritual history and forms an important primary text, as well, for Christian ecospirituality. Francis is very careful to direct his praise both to the family members of sun, moon, wind, water, fire, and earth and with them to God. The divine activity that creates and sustains all these parts of creation joins the activity of praise that Francis and these creatures offer to God. All of this energy is conjoined in the material world made sacred through this activity of being, sustaining, and praising. Rather than divinizing creation, which is an approach taken by pantheists who see all of creation as divine, Francis's song of praise expresses a very strong panentheism, in which everything is seen as being in God. All the activities of the material world are activated by God's sustaining activity and seen thus as manifestations of God, as thoroughly saturated with divine being. This panentheistic approach to understanding creation preserves God's radical and seemingly paradoxical transcendence and immanence, the apophatic unknown unexpressed with the kataphatic exuberance of doxology expressed in the canticle itself.

Painters and sculptors have long taken Francis as their subject, and in very contemporary art works, Francis often embodies the human in its cosmic dimension as a member of a larger world seen as pervaded by divine presence. See, for instance, artist Michael Divine's *Recognition (The Compassion of St. Francis)*, in which Francis is not the only figure with an iconic halo indicating sanctity. His companion animals of birds, butterflies, a rabbit, a deer, and a fox also have haloes or are encircled by and creating sacred space. Michael Divine may be pointing to Francis's compassion as the work's title indicates, but the painting also demonstrates shared dimensions of being between human and nonhuman identities. See also artist Marcy Hall's *Francis of Assisi*, which is part of her *Abbey of the Arts Dancing Monks* series, as Francis playfully cavorts across her colorful icon with a fox, birds, and fish. Across the top of the image are the words "The World Is My Monastery," which indicate the openness to divine presence Francis found in the world where he might have mingled contemplative prayer with action for social justice. His was a spirituality of going in and going without as reciprocal and reinforcing actions. Relying on the hospitality of strangers as a mendicant monk, or one who owned nothing and begged for his living, Francis not only subverted reliance on and participation within the common economic models of prosperity as a mode of being that enslaves one to one's own desires and the marketplace; he also modeled the radical freedom and joy experienced by one liberated from their own compulsions and market manipulation.

Pope Francis took his papal name from this very important saint, and Pope Francis's encyclical on creation care, an authoritative document in the Roman Catholic Church, draws its name from the opening words of Francis's canticle: *laudato si'*, or "praise be to you." In the opening paragraphs of the encyclical, Pope Francis names Sister Mother Earth, in imitation of Francis of Assisi, as calling out for all the pain inflicted upon her by human beings. Throughout the encyclical, Pope Francis evokes his readers' attentive listening and responding to both the cries of the poor and the cries of the earth, drawing our attention to the ways in which social justice and ecojustice converge. In explaining his respect for Francis, the pope writes,

> Saint Francis is the example par excellence of care for the vulnerable and of an integral ecology lived out joyfully and authentically. He is the patron saint of all who study and work in the area of ecology, and he is also much loved by non-Christians. He was particularly concerned for God's creation and for the poor and outcast. He loved, and was deeply loved for his joy, his generous self-giving, his openheartedness. He was a mystic and a pilgrim who lived in simplicity and in wonderful harmony with God, with others, with nature and with himself. He shows us just how inseparable the bond is between concern for nature, justice for the poor, commitment to society, and interior peace.[5]

Franciscans today may squirm when they think about the romanticized version of Francis so common in popular culture that focuses on Francis's experience of harmony with nature without taking into account his radical commitment to justice for the poor, sick, and marginalized—a commitment that may in fact call for significant restraint and sacrifice on our part when our privilege enables us to live in ways that compound their poverty, illness, and marginalization. This too accompanies Francis's call for radical solidarity with the oppressed and for coming awake to our own roles in being complicit among oppressors. It may feel difficult today to think of how to emulate Francis's life when one does not see oneself comfortably preaching to birds and mediating a conflict with predator wildlife in the ways of Saint Francis. But one can enter into relationships with the natural world that help one live in it and make decisions to benefit the well-being of those other-than-human creatures with whom we share this planet Earth.

As one example, contemporary writer Belden Lane, in his book *The Great Conversation*, describes a large tree in his neighborhood park that he comes to know as Grandfather Cottonwood.[6] This tree provides companionship throughout the year as Lane visits the park with his own granddaughter and rests in the shade of the tree, climbs the tree's branches, and even sits within a gash in the trunk created by a lightning strike. Lane's experience is a bit unusual. Not many of us would develop quite so *familiar* a relationship with a plant member of the Earth community as Lane does with this tree. And yet, Lane charts his own inner transformation as he forms this strong relationship of attachment and even love with the tree that evokes the possibilities for our own transformations. He describes a typology of spiritual change that involves recognition of one's position as user (exploiting nature) and then moves to explorer (yielding to fascination with nature), to celebrant (experiencing awe and praise of nature), and finally to lover (seeking union with nature). Lane's final stage draws from the mystical itinerary in Christian and other wisdom spiritual traditions and might more appropriately be described as ecomysticism. However, he acknowledges—and we can as well—that he never becomes *one* with the tree, though he enters it the way Jonah entered the fish. Relationships of love are characterized by presence within differentiation so that two are as close as possible while respecting and affirming their differences. Lane is pointing to a reality that is already ours but just needs conscious recognition so that it informs our actions. We *are* a part of the natural world already.

To express this just a little bit differently, we might experiment with adopting the image of the philosopher of Buddhism and Taoism, Alan Watts, who suggested thinking of the universe as a tree. We humans then are not separate, like birds living in the tree's branches. Rather, a different sense of identity, relationship, and responsibility is evoked when we think of humans as the leaves growing out of the branches of the tree (or universe). Watts claims, "We do not 'come into' this world; we come out of it, as leaves from a tree. As the ocean 'waves,' the universe 'peoples.' Every individual is an expression of the whole realm of nature, a unique action of the total universe."[7] This sense of union and interrelatedness could yield quite easily to our new regard for species with whom we share this planet Earth. What if we were to form a bond with the plants and animals in our neighborhoods, in our yards, in our homes? We might provide better care for those to whom we've pledged care, but we might also be changed beyond our wildest imaginings. Many of us might regard our cats and dogs as family members quite readily, but can we do as much for the pests or predators that annoy or threaten us? Could we remind ourselves that most families hold tensions, resolved and unresolved? And when we have had troubled or abusive relationships within families, could not the Earth community become a place where we find home and belonging, acceptance and love—that is, family?

Pope Francis indicates that the harmony Francis of Assisi experienced with creation represents a healing of the rupture between humans and other-than-humans described in the second creation account in Genesis.[8] It might also represent a healing of the rupture between humans themselves that was also indicated in the Genesis account. Relationships of domination and exploitation between humans and the rest of creation and between male and female humans seem to be endorsed by divine authority in these biblical narratives. Our experiences of creation care now, in the ways that Francis modeled, can facilitate our healing the ruptures we, too, may experience between one another and between ourselves and the natural world that is our home. By creating the conditions for healthy relationships with others and with all of creation, we effect what Pope Francis calls an ecological conversion: we recognize our errors, we repent, we experience anew a desire to change,[9] and most importantly, we do the work that constitutes change. In this way, we situate ourselves not only as responsible citizens of the global community but as grateful participants in an Earth community that relies on our using our own unique gifts for the well-being and flourishing of all.

HILDEGARD:
A SISTER FOR ALL SEASONS

Just as Francis is a figure whom modern-day artists take as a subject to explore and express relationships within the sacred Earth community, so Hildegard may be seen as a subject suitable for expressing understanding of the "greenness" she celebrated as present throughout the natural world. A modern iconographer, William Hart McNichols, created an icon that groups Francis and Hildegard with Jesus and Ignatius of Loyola. Other Earth images of leaves and stones surround a central image of Earth in McNichols's work. McNichols calls this icon *Viriditas: Finding God in All Things*, pairing a central concept from Hildegard's work with the Ignatian motto indicating a method of discernment. Notably in this icon, Earth is encircled with a bold green line indicating Hildegard's notion of *viriditas*. Traces of reddish color in many of the panels' images indicate life-giving blood of wounds and of healing that *viriditas* might occasion. This is a work that acknowledges the significance of these three figures from the Christian spiritual tradition as having a common vision of the sacredness of creation.

Hildegard (1098–1179) was a Benedictine who lived just before Francis's time. She was pledged from childhood to a monastic life and grew up in a community setting in which Benedictine spiritual practice was prioritized. She also grew up in a setting where she could learn about the natural world and the medicinal and healing qualities of plants in the monastic gardens she and her friends tended. As she united this experience with her theological training, she grew to formulate an understanding of the Holy Spirit's operation throughout all creation as a kind of green power she named *viriditas*. This power was in fact the power to *make* green those aspects of the natural world withered or dry, even dying—to, in fact, bring them back to life in a way that only the sacred and life-giving in creation can. The cyclic pattern of drying out and refreshing, even of dying and coming back to life, was a pattern that Hildegard understood was facilitated by *viriditas*.

Hildegard, in addition to being an herbalist and drawing on the natural world to heal, was an artist, musician, and composer. A film about her life, *Vision*, reveals poignantly her own debilitating experience with what might now be diagnosed as migraines but that Hildegard believed was a part of her spiritual identity of being stricken by awe of a powerful, living light she was able to see from a very young age. Though experience of this living light was painful, it also rendered her open to prophetic understanding often communicated by symbolic images that her writings interpret. An artist and writer, she married image and word to convey the meanings she understood her visions to give her for healing and restoration.

In the opening of her visions, Hildegard describes the simultaneous wounding and gifting of her embodied condition: "Heaven was opened and a fiery light of exceeding brilliance came and permeated my whole brain, and inflamed my whole heart and my whole breast, not like a burning but like a warming flame, as the sun warms anything its rays touch." Then Hildegard heard, "I am the Living Light, Who illuminates the darkness. The person whom I have chosen and whom I have miraculously stricken as I willed, I have placed among great wonders, beyond the measure of the ancient people who saw in Me many secrets; but I have laid her low on the earth, that she might not set herself up in arrogance of mind."[10] This humility to which Hildegard was subjected by these visions paradoxically also opened up new vistas of experience and understanding of her place as a human within the setting of the larger created universe.

Hildegard's vision of the universe is noteworthy among many visions contained in her *Scivias* (a word functioning as shorthand for *Scito vias Domini*, or "know the ways of the Lord"), a work she illuminated. The vision of the universe figures as the third vision in *Scivias* and is illuminated, and the illumination is interpreted in short paragraphs attending to visual details of the image. Notably the "universe" is imaged as a close-up detail of a woman giving birth, with imagery of a woman's generative organs ornately manifesting an egg-shaped universe that Hildegard must have regarded as profoundly generative via the *viriditas* or greening power throughout the universe. When interpreting humanity's placement within the universe, Hildegard does sometimes express herself in anthropocentric terms consistent with her time period, and yet her explanation of the vision also alludes to an embeddedness within creation that all of humanity shares. She describes it as follows:

And in the midst of these elements is a sandy globe of great magnitude, which these elements have so surrounded that it cannot waver in any direction. This openly shows that, of all the strengths of God's creation, Man's [or the Human Being's] is most profound, made in a wondrous way with great glory from the dust of the earth and so entangled with the strengths of the rest of creation that [this being] can never be separated from them; for the elements of the world, created for [Humanity's] service, wait upon [Humanity], and [Humanity], enthroned as it were in their midst, by divine disposition presides over them.[11]

Certainly, this description could troublingly convey the theme of dominion so prevalent in Judeo-Christian traditions and interpreted to authorize domination and exploitation, and yet Hildegard's vision tempers the human exceptionalism that might be drawn from this passage when she writes of the strengths of all parts of God's creation. There may indeed be ways that humanity regards its own strength as "most profound" of all such strengths, but Hildegard's vision of the entanglements of these strengths means that building a hierarchy that places humanity at the top would subvert the sense of biocentrism her vision of *viriditas* affirms. Indeed, we can probably see how the temptation to move immediately to anthropocentric bias, given our understanding of a privileged position of strength in the universe, immediately obscures the kinship and belonging Francis described that was ideal for humanity to experience. This temptation to celebrate one's own powers unjustly, or at the expense of other creatures' strengths, could itself be seen as a wounding of humanity and, in fact, humanity's deepest, most pressing wound.

Hildegard believed, like others of her time period, in the efficacy of not only nature but also music to heal. As a composer and musician, she wrote lyrics that celebrate the healing qualities of God at work in the natural world. For instance, she wrote this song to the Holy Spirit:

Holy Spirit, making life alive,
moving in all things, root of all created being,
cleansing the cosmos of every impurity, effacing guilt,
anointing wounds.

You are lustrous and praiseworthy life,
You awaken and re-awaken everything that is.[12]

In this song, Hildegard declares the power of the Holy Spirit to be the source and sustainer of all things ("root" and "moving"), and she affirms this sacred spirit's cleansing and healing properties. The awakening and reawakening the song concludes with reflect the opening line of making life live. Hildegard humbly points to this sacred divine element in all things that is responsible for the life similarly coursing through the veins in our bodies and the veins in a leaf. Many of her other lyrics celebrate greenness as applied to the soul, to specific people like Mary, the mother of Jesus, and to members of Hildegard's monastic community.

John Dadosky helpfully draws Hildegard's notion of *viriditas* into conversation with Pope Francis's encyclical on creation care, *Laudato si'*, reminding us that Pope Francis's encyclical, though rich in theory and practical advice, draws primarily from masculine voices in spiritual traditions, both Christian and otherwise. Hildegard's voice helpfully complements what is lacking in the encyclical in directing our attention to God's power to restore to wholeness a world whose integrity is compromised due to anthropocentric activity. While Pope Francis diagnoses and describes this condition, calling out our anthropocentrism and inviting us to biocentrism, Hildegard's conviction—drawn from her experience that *viriditas* forms the basis of our being and becoming—can move us into a sensibility more in line with Pope Francis's and that of all people of goodwill whom his encyclical addresses.

In the third chapter of the encyclical, for instance, Pope Francis diagnoses the human roots of ecological crisis and describes such devastations to the natural world as biodiversity loss, desertification, and destruction of forests, coral reefs, and glaciers—these can be seen as losses of *viriditas* in the natural world.[13] Hildegard's natural remedy is to experience and understand a common power of greening to pervade all that is, our own human bodies as well as our natural human homes and neighbors. This common sacred power anticipated the kinship celebrated by Francis, as both saints recognized a common sacred source and sustainer in the energy by which all creation is maintained in being.

CONCLUSION

Icons have traditionally been important tools in Christian spiritual life and in spiritual transformation because they help us understand who we are and who we want to become by expressing the value we affirm in our ancestors in faith. Icons do this principally through affirmations of beauty. Perhaps most notably, images of Jesus alive and ministering and dying on the cross have functioned for centuries for Christians desirous of being reminded of the dying-to-oneself that a Christian is meant to do in following Jesus's way of life. In an era when our imaginations are often caught by the visual storytelling of television shows and movies, it might be helpful to consider how we engage visual media. Are the stories and the characters we engage in these shows and movies ones that help us understand our place of belonging within the natural world? Do they help us heal our own wounds or the wounds in our communities? When thinking of how humans differ from other creatures, human reason, imagination, and empathy are often cited as qualities unique to humans. If this is so, how are we best using such "strengths" to further the project of well-being and flourishing that we and our more-than-human neighbors deserve? How are we engaging the arts and our own creative powers for healing?

Francis's song of praise for the natural world elaborated his understanding of creation kinship and helped plant his feet squarely in a community of family larger than the human society in which he was born and which to some extent he rejected and was rejected by because of his biological family's and his society's focus on materialistic excess facilitated by inattention to the sick and the poor. Hildegard's elaboration of *viriditas* in her treatises and songs underscores her understanding of God's sacred restorative power as operating throughout creation and without which nothing could exist. These two thinkers and their experiential engagement of the natural world as the site of our most profound belonging and healing are seeds that, sown in our understanding, may reweave our experiences of belonging and healing into the natural world in our own times. Not accustomed, perhaps, to thinking of members of the Earth community as family, we would do well to recover this kinship and to celebrate the ways in which the natural world replenishes us when our energies dip.

Questions for Reflection and Discussion

- Where would you place yourself on the scale suggested by Lane: user, explorer, celebrant, or lover of nature? What specific actions do you associate with each of these levels?
- Have you ever experienced familial kinship with an animal or plant? What circumstances allowed you to have that understanding of your relationship? What might make it possible for you to have or enhance such relationships of kinship?
- What places in nature most readily evoke your expressions of love, awe, and praise? How often are you able to be in those places? What in your daily circumstances might, if attentively engaged, facilitate your belonging and your healing?
- Francis often spoke lovingly of Lady Poverty. In what way might simple living and frugality be an expression of our love for the natural world? Do you, in fact, value these things? And if so, how do you live them?
- Pope Francis's encyclical mentions ecological conversion. What would it take for you to convert (literally, turn around) to a new way of expressing your life in the world and relationships with others?

Suggested Ecospiritual Practices

Meditate with and reflect on the opening lines of Galway Kinnell's "Saint Francis and the Sow."[14] In this poem, Kinnell writes of activities of self-blessing when we recognize that there is something in us that is our sacred source and sustenance that, in turn, sustains others. What is that for you? When have you experienced it? Practice going about your day with a heightened sensitivity to your being a blessing to others and to your receiving others as blessings. Reflect at the end of the day on what changes in your behavior and thought patterns you noticed because of this intention. Consider this an invitation to acknowledge, accept, and appreciate your own loveliness and ability to love and be loved, to bless and to be blessed.

Francis loved poverty. While we do not want to romanticize the experience of being without the things we legitimately need, we should consider how privileged many of us are in terms of our access to not only things we need but things we want. Do a small inventory of things immediately around you: How many are necessary or superfluous? How much do you yourself value simplicity or frugality? In what areas of your life might you experience the beauty of a simpler way of doing things or of owning fewer things? Games? Books? Food? If you need a bit of extra motivation to see the beauty of simplicity and how it might be a means to a more flourishing form of life for you and others, research the materials or means of production for some of the things in your life. Were they ethically sourced? Were people paid a living wage to make and sell them? Consider this an invitation to begin to make decisions about what is in your life that contributes to your and other beings' flourishing.

For Further Reading

Creation Spirituality: Liberating Gifts for the Peoples of the Earth by Matthew Fox (HarperCollins, 1991)

Laudato si' by Pope Francis, available online through the Vatican website

Loving Creation: Christian Spirituality, Earth-Centered and Just by Kathleen Fischer (Paulist, 2009)

Rooted and Rising: Voices of Courage in a Time of Climate Crisis edited by Leah D. Schade and Margaret Bullitt-Jonas (Rowman & Littlefield, 2019)

Saint Francis of Assisi: Brother of Creation by Mirabai Starr (Sounds True, 2013)

CHAPTER FOUR

Spiritualities of Stars and Soil

> Earth is what we all have in common.
> —Wendell Berry, *The Art of the Commonplace:*
> *The Agrarian Essays of Wendell Berry*

From looking at figures from late antiquity and the medieval period, we move now to our own past century and to two men whose experience of the natural world engaged their minds, bodies, and spirits in ways that "seed" ongoing ecotheological reflection and eco-spiritual practice. Thomas Berry (1914–2009) and Wendell Berry (1934–present), unrelated though sharing the same last name, both worked as writers in the genres of essay and poetry, while Wendell Berry also wrote novels and short stories. Both men sought to interpret their experiences of awe and gratitude toward the natural world in ways that might recover human identity and community within the local and global contexts in which individual human and more-than-human lives flourish. Though they represent a privileged position in terms of both being white American males, their taking a countercultural stance on cultivation of a land ethic and rein-vention of the human entailed their countering a toxic masculinity endemic to the North American culture in which they were formed. For this reason, they are instructive exemplars of the ecospiritual life as they lived in ways contrary to the so-called American dream and raised critical questions about their own cultural and religious priv-ilege and the anthropocentric perspective that is typically associated with that privilege. Similarly, both men addressed gender and racial discrimination in their work as they critiqued norms and inspired their readers to value relationality and the life that people of differing genders might create together and to undermine assumptions of ethnic superiority historically expressed in occupation of American lands and slavery.

Thomas Berry contributed to a new understanding of the human story set within the continuity of larger and longer stories of the universe, of the planet Earth, and of life on Earth.[1] Though in many ways very grounded in his approach to ecospirituality, Thomas Berry's vocational task was to set our human experience of life in the context of these other stories in which human consciousness expresses a universe come to consciousness and self-reflection in a way that invites human dignity and responsibility. Thomas Berry's eyes were on the stars as he recovered a cosmological narrative within which to coax human consciousness and sensibility to unfold meaningfully. Human bodies share ancestral materials of hydrogen, helium, carbon, nitrogen, oxygen, and iron with other forms of life on Earth. Berry's visionary representation of human and life transformation meant he was peculiarly well suited to articulate a reinvention of the human at this time in human history and to espouse new ways we might live to facilitate human flourishing.

Wendell Berry, on the other hand, is a farmer who realized the importance for him of his homeland in Kentucky and the importance for every person to have a restored relationship to the bioregion within which their identities and characters were formed and to which they owe a fundamental fidelity. Wendell Berry draws inspiration for his essays, poetry, and fiction from his particular place and his experience of home and working closely with land that he cultivates and with the companion animals who help him best serve the land. His life as a farmer embodies an intimate presence with and respect for soil and all that soil signifies for the thriving of human and more-than-human members of the Earth community. In addition, Wendell Berry's fiction and nonfiction regularly critique economies that put small household farms out of business, and he argues that something important about human dignity and responsibility is lost when we no longer have an opportunity to get our own hands in the dirt. Unlike Thomas Berry, who was a Catholic priest who took vows in the Passionist Order, Wendell Berry is a husband and a father, and his social sense of community emerged from his own experience of family in a way that differs from Thomas Berry's lived experience as a priest with many friends and students with whom he formed community.

Thomas Berry and Wendell Berry have each done something significant in discerning the seeds of their traditions, Catholic and Protestant, respectively, to blossom and fruit in their own lives as a commitment to relate to the sacred by way of creature kin of animals, plants, and cosmic elements. As each thinker describes his profound experience of the natural world as a young person who seeded his lifelong practices of respect, care, and love for the natural world, I urge you to consider your own story. Where did you first notice aspects of the natural world with wonder, awe, gratitude, concern? When did this happen in your life? What facilitated this experience, in terms of your being in the presence of certain other-than-human members of the Earth community, using your imagination to consider another being's viewpoint, or feeling empathy for another being? These particular experiences formed Thomas Berry and Wendell Berry into the deep and generous thinkers they became, and your own experience catalyzes for you what is most important about your own engagement with your unique setting, shared with others.

These men's lives and practices also suggest important ways we might activate our own awareness of human identity in continuity with other creaturely companions with whom we share a universe home and might deepen our awareness of our intimate relationships with those in closest proximity to us in our own bioregions, homelands, and watersheds. These two men together represent a balanced polarity of experience and reflection centered in the stars of a universe and in the soil of our own planet Earth.

THOMAS BERRY:
COSMOLOGIST AND GEOLOGIAN

Thomas Berry considered himself a "geologian" rather than a theologian, for he recognized that the content of his discourse (his "logos") was more often the earth (geo-) than God (theo-). Further, he worked tirelessly to eliminate a distinction between the two, drawing on the thought of the Catholic thinker Thomas Aquinas, whose first name he adopted as his own when making vows within religious life. However, Thomas Berry's worldview arose invariably from his training in the history of religions, as he brought his Catholic upbringing into conversation with the traditions of Hinduism, Taoism, and Buddhism.[2] For a very brief while, Thomas Berry lived in China, and his ongoing engagement with sacred texts of these traditions remained influential on his thought as he taught the history of religions at Fordham University and then established the Riverdale Center for Religious Research in Riverdale, New York. This center gave Berry a home from which to offer seminars and to collaborate in discussions with students and other scholars trying to understand how differing cultures enact harmony with the natural world and respond to the exigencies of their own times, unfolding in crises and conflicts as moments of renewal and transformation. This response to the needs of one's time is the "great work" that became the title of an important book by Thomas Berry. The great work of our time, Berry could see, was going to be confronting climate change and helping our cultural systems assimilate this contemporary reality and the larger cosmological narrative that this moment contributes to, especially to activate a response that is meaningful on behalf of the whole of the Earth community and not just the survival of human beings.

The Riverdale Center also gave Thomas Berry physical space to store and share numerous volumes of sacred texts from world religious traditions, from which his own work drew. As he sought to widen the parameters of his own faith community to larger understandings of human identity, he began to bring his understanding of a cosmological identity to bear on his work. His predecessor in this work was another Catholic, the Jesuit paleontologist Pierre Teilhard de Chardin (1881–1955), whose understanding of science and religion enabled him to articulate in a very succinct and creative manner how human beings developed in continuity with the universe itself—much as Alan Watts did using the image of a tree with leaves, mentioned in the previous chapter. Thomas Berry understood himself as within the context of the human community and able to make the following definition: "The human is that being in whom the universe reflects on and celebrates itself and its numinous origin in its own, unique mode of conscious self-awareness."³ Rather than diminish the human species, this definition emphasizes the place of belonging that humans share with all that is and the unique gifts of awareness—and related gifts—that the universe has expressed by bringing humans into being. In Watts's words, the universe "peoples."

Most importantly, Berry returns in his work to a transformative moment in his childhood when he understood fundamental values to emerge from his perception of a field of wildflowers. He described this experience in his book *The Great Work* as a "magic moment," one that fundamentally shaped the rest of his life at what he calls a "more profound level" than any other experience.⁴ Berry then goes on to explain the worldview that emerged from this experience by claiming the field accrued some authority in his life by virtue of its existing and thriving quite independently of Berry's own involvement with the field. He realized, "Whatever preserves or enhances this meadow in the natural cycles of its transformation is good; whatever opposes this meadow or negates it is not good."⁵ In line with Aldo Leopold's "land ethic," Berry understood the rights of this particular place to be just as valid as the rights of other places and that each place has rights to exist and to flourish. This Earth jurisprudence continues to bear fruit in the work of legal advisors working to reframe various countries' constitutions and bodies of legislative documents to affirm the rights of important members of our Earth community such as rivers, mountains, and forests. Berry claimed, "These evolving biosystems deserve the opportunity to be themselves and to express their own inner qualities. As in economics, so in jurisprudence and law and political affairs—what is good recognizes the rights of this meadow and the creek and the woodlands beyond to exist and flourish in their ever-renewing seasonal expression even while larger processes shape the bioregion in its sequence of transformations."[6]

From this early experience of recognition, Berry went on to religious life with a particular Catholic order called the Passionists, and he expanded his field of study from religious traditions and their cosmologies (or creation stories) to include the scientific story of origins as it was coming to be known during his lifetime. Theories like the "big bang" that described possible ways to envision the origin of the universe so gripped his imagination that he came to believe that humans needed these cosmological narratives to shape our sense of and understanding of ourselves and to give us our sense of purpose and significance within the larger scheme of things. It is no accident, he believed, that every religious tradition has some narrative describing cosmic origins. Berry met Brian Swimme at the Riverdale Center, where Swimme had come to study, and together they collaborated on a project to articulate the universe story, offering a perspective that unites scientific and religious worldviews in a narrative that explains both the *how* and the *why* of what might have occurred during what Berry preferred to call a great "flaring forth" rather than a "big bang" and what has happened since. Within the context of this universe story, Thomas Berry's most important statements to which he returned in many of his writings and which seed his own students' writings are the following:

The universe is a communion of subjects, not a collection of objects.[7] By this, Thomas Berry meant to subvert the anthropocentrism of our human perspective that objectifies the rest of the world by centering our own subjectivity. We thus justify our own uses, misuses, and abuses of the rest of the world. To correct this, Berry countered with a perspective that emphasizes communion, calling our immediate context an Earth community that humans share with plants, other animals, and the features of our home of belonging, such as mountains, plains, bodies of water, jungles, forests, and deserts. Each of these, like the meadow he encountered as a young person, have their own subjectivity, or their own lives, with which we too, with our own subjectivity, are entangled. Two perspectives that counter anthropocentrism are geocentrism, centering the planet's subjectivity, and biocentrism, centering life more generally. By recovering a sense of human membership in community, Berry hoped to alleviate some of the species loneliness he intuited we were heading for and already prone to. To counter a spirituality of alienation, his principle of a community of subjects corresponds to a spirituality of intimacy.[8] Further, Thomas Berry proposed a novel revaluation of hierarchy to effect this spirituality of intimacy. While others might try to correct and circumvent the injustices aligned with hierarchies that allow one group to dominate over others by eliminating hierarchy altogether or by inverting hierarchies, putting marginalized groups at the center or top, Berry proposed a universalizing of hierarchy. He wrote of the particularity or gifts of each part of creation, "Regarding egalitarianism and hierarchy, I suggest that, rather than diminish hierarchy, we universalize it. Everything is at the top of the hierarchy in its own way. When it comes to swimming, the fish are at the top. When it comes to flying, the birds are at the top. When it comes to bearing peaches, peach trees are at the top. When it comes to being a person's own specific self, that person is at the top."[9] This suggestion invites us to celebrate the unique contribution each part of the Earth community, ourselves included, makes to the functioning and flourishing of all.

The universe is the primary revelation of the sacred.[10] To some people, this statement may sound pantheistic and contrary to Berry's Christian orientation. Nevertheless, Berry wanted to stress the importance of the universe as revealing the sacred, or God for theists, rather than focus on revelation in a written text like the Bible; remember that he advised that people put aside the Bible for a while until they recovered this very important sensibility. Berry believed that the universe was in fact the only text with no context, whereas the Bible is a text with context (the human community reading it within the context of the whole universe), and for this reason, the universe should be "read" attentively by its inhabitants so as to understand the creator better.

Such a reading, however, expands the parameters of what humans mean by language and expression, decentering an emphasis on the human word for communication by recognizing that other beings speak by virtue of their being. Other religious traditions speak of being and expression, for instance, in the terms "a cloud *clouds*" or "a tree *trees*."[11] Again, Berry is suggesting that we celebrate the diverse ways that life is expressed—reminding us that intuitions of the sacred emerge through all these ways that life is expressed and shared.

The sacred is that which evokes the depths of wonder.[12] Finally, conscious of the differences between religious and cultural traditions and yet cognizant of commonalities between them, Berry strove for expansive articulations of who God might be and how God might be apprehended. When defining the sacred, then, he chose to focus on that which evokes awe and wonder, which for many may be God, and yet most of these evocations occur as encounters with the natural world, with beauty, with something that draws us not only "out of ourselves" (the meaning of ecstasy) but also even more deeply into ourselves. Berry would likely have agreed with feminist theologian Daphne Hampson when she described God as "that through which we come to be most fully ourselves."[13]

When I wrote in the introduction to this chapter about Thomas Berry being grounded, I meant to suggest that he and Wendell Berry are not as polarizing as I make them out to be in their vision of comprehensive experience this chapter investigates. As we turn to Wendell Berry's "seeds" of wisdom for ecospirituality, I conclude by aligning Thomas Berry's recognition of what radical transformations are needed on the ground—in the world where our bodies reside, and not among the stars—to which he was particularly attuned and which, in many ways, he characterized as the "great work" to which living generations today should be devoted, with Wendell Berry's work. These are specific actions such as "organic farming, community-supported agriculture, solar-hydrogen energy system, redesign of our cities, elimination of the automobile in its present form, restoration of local village economies, education for a post-petroleum way of life, and a jurisprudence that recognizes the rights of natural modes of being."[14]

These are actions that one readily discerns in Wendell Berry's work as needed for the future we hope we may live into.

WENDELL BERRY: PHILOSOPHER AND FARMER

Just as Thomas Berry described a transformative moment of engaging the natural world and enjoying its beauty, purpose, and value quite apart from his own human need or use of it, so Wendell Berry writes of a "native hill" that made such a deep impression on him that he kept the hill's memory with him always, as it proved consoling and irresistible. He writes,

> In my teens, when I was away at school, I could comfort myself by recalling in intricate detail the fields I had worked and played in, and hunted over, and ridden through on horseback—and that they were richly associated in my mind with people and with stories. I could recall even the casual locations of certain small rocks. I could recall the look of a hundred different kinds of daylight on all those places, the look of animals grazing over them, the postures and attitudes and movements of the men who worked in them, the quality of the grass and the crops that had grown on them. I had come to be aware of it as one is aware of one's body; it was present to me whether I thought of it or not.[15]

This native space was the land he eventually farmed and lived on for most of his life, reclaiming the life and work of his forebears after a brief, unsatisfying foray into academic life in a city. It was important to Berry that he have a relationship with the soil from which comes our essential sustenance. The loss of this relationship seems, in Wendell Berry's writings, to constitute a grievous loss of our identity and purpose—and one that many others might grieve, suffering a loss of connection with lands our ancestors may have farmed and cared for as well. Berry believed that we all can live more closely with the soil that sustains us, even if such closeness seems curtailed by urban life. Not all of us can farm, certainly. But the springing up of urban farms and of farmers' markets indicates a real hunger in human experience to reconnect with the fundamental truth of human and Earth connection. Throughout his writings, fiction and nonfiction, Wendell Berry returns to some fundamental truths about human life that he draws from his ongoing intimacy with the land that he cultivated and the soil whose being sustained him. He writes poignantly of the space that felt as familiar as a family member, using anthropomorphism or personification to express this intimacy: "The hill is like an old woman, all her human obligations met, who sits at work day after day, in a kind of rapt leisure, at an intricate embroidery. She has time for all things. Because she does not expect ever to be finished, she is endlessly patient with details. She perfects flower and leaf, feather and song, adorning the briefest life in great beauty as though it were meant to last forever."[16]

Of course, it is quite common to see Earth personified as a woman in this way. But not quite so common to see her as a woman who takes her time with things, as Berry represents her here. Some feminists object to the drawing together of feminine imagery in nature because it forecloses the identification of women with the production of culture, an activity seen primarily as men's work. Others, though, celebrate the identification, claiming it helps to render clearer the exploitation of women and nature that comes from life-giving (via birth and food) associated with women and land. Here, Berry is celebrating the work of a woman, likely drawing on family members or members of his community whom he knew as patient older women, content with sitting at leisure, working, and spending a great deal of time and effort on things that maybe many of us would disdain, such as the beauty of wild places, especially places unconducive to human habitation or unproductive in response to human cultivation. Wendell Berry sees the world of the land and of the sacred as being so gratuitously attentive to detail and to elaborate perfection that in human consciousness, it seems all the more gratuitous and even unnecessary given the temporary nature of most natural things and even human life. It would seem clear from this quote that Wendell Berry would object to any trivialization of our natural lives here on Earth and to the mistreatment of any part of the natural landscape overlooked and made negligible because of human focus on profit, production, and even exploitation. Some of the seeds of his wisdom for ecospirituality include the following:

Human limits are worth celebrating. Wendell Berry's attention to the human person dealt not with the celebrating of technological advances made possible through human ingenuity but with the wisdom that humans have to relinquish control made possible through human invention. We have a paradoxical opportunity to divest ourselves of the power to which we have access in order to restore the balance between human flourishing and the flourishing of the more-than-human world. To this end, we need to restore respect for limits, and part of that respect means acknowledging the cyclical nature of human life, entailing growth and decrepitude, living and dying—cycles that we saw earlier that Hildegard understood as negotiated by means of *viriditas*, or green power. Berry wrote, "In the cycles of farming, which carry the elemental energy again and again through the seasons and the bodies of living things, we recognize the only infinitude within reach of the imagination."[17] The soil with which a farmer or gardener works evokes the reality of "to dust we return." Further, Berry claims that it is essential that we recognize and respect the limits to human living or we may not survive at all. He writes, "It is more likely that we will have either to live within our limits, within the human definition, or not live at all. And certainly the knowledge of these limits and of how to live within them is the most comely and graceful knowledge that we have, the most healing and the most whole."[18] Though an unpopular notion, restraint or self-discipline appears as a principle by which human flourishing and the flourishing of all creation is made possible. Other writers focus on dependency, contingency, vulnerability, and even precariousness to elaborate this notion of human experience that today is more vital than ever to recover.

Earth care is a beautiful human responsibility. When we think of human identity, Thomas Berry elaborates a vision of the human in continuity with all creation and emerging as a feature of the universe newly come to consciousness and self-awareness. Wendell Berry's sensibility focuses on the respite that creation offers humanity and the human response engendered from enjoyment of that respite. He writes, "The care of the earth is our most ancient and most worthy and, after all, our most pleasing responsibility. To cherish what remains of it, and to foster its renewal, is our only legitimate hope."[19] Rather than contributing to our current economic system that requires and rewards productivity and allows us leisure only when profitable to the interests of the corporations that consider us merely producers and consumers, Wendell Berry instead welcomes us to an urgent task of creation care that attends to our vital needs for dignity, meaning, purpose, value, relationship, and connectedness. Avoidance of work does not actually contribute to our sense of well-being, however much we may relish and desire vacations in tropical places. On the contrary, work that has meaning initiates us into rhythms appropriate to our human identity—rhythms of work, rest, and play that truly restore us as human beings within our Earth community.

The peace of wild things restores humanity to itself. Wendell Berry's poems are various and contain much imagery of the natural world in both its cultivated and wild forms, with which he is deeply familiar. One of his most beloved poems is this:

When despair for the world grows in me
and I wake in the night at the least sound
in fear of what my life and my children's lives may be,
I go and lie down where the wood drake
rests in his beauty on the water, and the great heron feeds.
I come into the peace of wild things
who do not take their lives with forethought
of grief. I come into the presence of still water.
And I feel above me the day-blind stars

waiting with their light. For a time
I rest in the grace of the world, and am free.[20]

Like in the quotation about his recognition of the patient work of
the "native hill," in this poem, Wendell Berry is celebrating a place
where true peace can be found because no "forethought" is engaged
by these other neighbors with whom Berry shares a home. In those
places, he can set aside his despair, his fear, his anxiety, and the expectations he likely feels projected onto him by the world in terms of his
own production value and the toxic masculinity expected of him as a
white male relating to others, human and more-than-human. These
patterns of being disrupt the social fabric and render him unable to
live into his fullest being and to act within membership of the Earth
community. It is here that a peacefulness exudes and thus enables his
recovery. As Chellis Glendinning famously entitled her classic of eco-
psychology, *My Name Is Chellis and I'm in Recovery from Western Civilization* (Shambhala, 1994), Wendell Berry also felt that the recovery
of one's relationship with land might provide an antidote to western
civilization and its normative values.

Early on in his career as a farmer and poet, Wendell Berry made
a regular practice of writing poems on the Sabbath, which Christians
observe as a day of rest on Sundays when they might go to church
or spend time with family members over a good meal or in the natural world. This practice of attending deeply to the holiness of a day
set aside for rest was Berry's way of recovering from western civilization, or at least the forms of it that cause the despair about which he
wrote in the first line of the poem above. He chose to practice this writing of poems on the Sabbath deliberately to be one of reflection and
being rather than doing, and many of his poems in this Sabbath series
express content that juxtaposes the work of the week with the repose
that humans need to experience not only as a restoration of their own
energies but also so that the natural world too might be relieved of
its time of being acted upon by human presence. Sabbath rest thus
becomes an opportunity for the inevitable impact of human presence
on the rest of the world to be withdrawn and relaxed and for us to

settle deliberately into a more respectful mode of being with the rest of the Earth community—which it is hoped might continue to inform our being during the remaining six days of the week. In these poems, such rest and contentment emerge as subversive. Sabbath rest afforded to humans, animals, and the land is biblical and draws from legislation in the Hebrew Scriptures (Exod 20:8–11 and Lev 25:2–7). Berry used his writing practice to embody this realization and, through careful elaboration of the relationship between human beings and the land, to remind himself and his readers that one relies essentially on this land and its soil for all our nourishment and well-being.

Here is one such Sabbath poem, of many, that represents Berry's deliberate cultivating of creativity and being rather than participating in the consumerist activity that characterizes so much of American and even global cultures:

> Whatever is foreseen in joy
> Must be lived out from day to day,
> Visions held open in the dark
> By our ten thousand days of work.
> Harvest will fill the barn; for that
> The hand must ache, the face must sweat.
>
> And yet no leaf or grain is filled
> By work of ours; the field is tilled
> And left to grace. That we may reap,
> Great work is done while we're asleep.
>
> When we work well, a Sabbath mood
> Rests on our day, and finds it good.[21]

CONCLUSION

Thomas Berry and Wendell Berry were men thoroughly attuned to dangerous trends in American life that prioritized convenience and even instant gratification over the patient and sometimes difficult work of maintaining relationships of respect and care. Thomas Berry saw the liabilities involved in religious traditions in conflict over cosmologies that contravened scientific accounts of life and human origins; he also was concerned to reinvigorate the story as a necessary component of human thriving and to enable humans to live their story against the backdrops of other stories—such as the American dream or dream of unlimited progress—within which human life is embedded. To fail to understand these comprehensive, interwoven stories was to have scientists pursuing one experience and understanding along a trajectory paralleled by another told by faith traditions—without the two coming together to articulate a common vision and purpose, giving a much-needed renewal of meaning to human life.

Wendell Berry experienced the tear in social fabrics on a small scale within rural communities fractured by large-scale farming enterprises. Agribusiness continues to dislocate farming families with practices that pollute land, air, and water and that exploit animals on a massive scale (an undercurrent of violence tolerated in many developed countries that links to interhuman violence). Most of his writings document this "unsettling" of American identity through this undermining of the familial and social communities living closely with the land.

The visionary experience of both men might be summed up by the British novelist and poet D. H. Lawrence when, diagnosing the human condition in the twentieth century and recommending a solution, he wrote, "We must get back into relation, vivid and nourishing relation to the cosmos and the universe. . . . For the truth is, we are perishing for lack of fulfillment of our greater needs, we are cut off from the great sources of our inward nourishment and renewal, sources which flow eternally in the universe. Vitally, the human race is dying. It is like a great uprooted tree, with its roots in the air. We must plant ourselves again in the universe."[22] This recommendation of rerooting ourselves works to unite the visions of Wendell and Thomas Berry, with one focused on the ground beneath our feet and the other seeking for a story of the human experience as originating within a massive universe over time becoming hospitable to human life. We need both visions and the ethics that emerge from such visions to recover the experience of ourselves as fundamentally a part of the natural world and to understand our purpose in celebrating the achievement of the universe in coming to conscious self-reflection in us and celebrating the gifts of imagination and empathy we can activate on behalf of our communities.

Questions for Reflection and Discussion

- How does Thomas Berry's definition of the sacred as that which evokes the depths of wonder compare with your own definition of the sacred?
- What do you consider the great work of your time? Does it have to do with human-divine relations, human-human relations, or human-Earth relations? What is your role to play in the great work of your generation?
- When have you had encounters like Thomas Berry's with a field of wildflowers or like Wendell Berry's with his native hill? What truths about life did that experience lead to? How would you tell the story of the impact of that encounter on your life?
- What do you do when despair for the world grows in you? Do you have places where you might imitate Wendell Berry's strategy for coping with and meeting such despair?
- Which of the principles described in this chapter and drawn from Thomas or Wendell Berry's thoughts most appeals to you, and why? Which is difficult to accept, and why? Is the Sabbath or other forms of rest something you can consciously create time for?

Suggested Ecospiritual Practices

Two activities of presence in the natural world are suggested by the lives, work, and ecospiritualities of Thomas Berry and Wendell Berry. The first is to stargaze. Spend some time outdoors in a space with little or no light pollution and experience your life story as in continuity with the universe story. How is your sense of the sacred spurred by such awesome recognition of long life in the stars and elsewhere in the cosmos? Rather than make you feel diminished by this activity of sensing your own insignificance in the grand scheme of things, how might this larger context in which your life is lived out give you the courage and resilience you might need right now? How might it give deeper meaning and purpose to your participation in the universe story and your contribution to the great work of our time? Consider this an invitation to experience the resonance of your own interior space of soul with that of the galaxy laid out to view just overhead.

The second activity is to get your hands dirty. Spend some time with your hands in the dirt, planting seeds or weeding a garden bed or transplanting a rootbound plant. Find out what plants thrive in the climate of your particular setting and learn how to care for them. If you can, plant vegetables or herbs from which you can harvest your own foods and grow in intimacy with your utter dependence on and vulnerability in regard to the natural world for nourishment, physical and spiritual. Your understanding of reliance on the natural world for sustenance will be enhanced, and your experience of satisfaction when caring for yourself as you care for plants that care for you will be phenomenal. Consider this an invitation to experience and foster your own caretaking capabilities, much needed in this time of ministering to the replenishing of the earth.

For Further Reading

Field of Compassion: How the New Cosmology Is Transforming Spiritual Life by Judy Cannato (Sorin, 2010)

Food and Faith: A Theology of Eating by Norman Wirzba (Cambridge University Press, 2020)

Liturgy of the Ordinary: Sacred Practices in Everyday Life by Tish Harrison Warren (InterVarsity, 2016)

Paradoxology: Spirituality in a Quantum Universe by Miriam Therese Winter (Orbis, 2009)

Quantum Theology: Spiritual Implications of the New Physics by Diarmuid O'Murchu (Crossroad, 2003)

CHAPTER FIVE

Greening Spiritual Practice

Our goal should be to live life in radical amazement, [to] get up in the morning and look at the world in a way that takes nothing for granted. Everything is phenomenal; everything is incredible. . . . To be spiritual is to be amazed.

—Abraham Joshua Heschel,
God in Search of Man: A Philosophy of Judaism

Every religious tradition has certain spiritual practices that serve to unify the members of the tradition. These practices may look similar across traditions when they function to preserve and enhance an individual's and a community's well-being. The motivation behind greening a spiritual practice evolves from a desire to integrate religious and ethical commitments with sociocultural experience, especially our contemporary experience of greater knowledge as to how our actions affect the natural world. In a way, religious or ethical commitments and one's sociocultural experience need not ever have been dissociated from one another, but in reality, they often have been. This means that people have more frequently been taught that holiness or devotion is more appropriate in a sacred setting like a church building or when doing things like praying or engaging in rituals or ceremonies. Whatever happened in that setting might not spill over into the life, values, purpose, or meaning of a person's life in other spaces, though it might have been intended to do so.

As Raimon Panikkar said of the Christian communion of which he was a part, "The purpose of the institution is to make transparent the experience that established it."[1] To make transparent, in fact, what first must have amazed the founder of any tradition: the sight of a burning bush, the opening of skies accompanied by a disembodied voice and the appearance of a bird, other appearances of angels and deities of all kinds. These are theophanies and geophanies of the finest sort, occasioning amazement and awe in those who first experienced them and occasioning the desire to communicate this experience to companions and subsequent communities of faith in order to enable others' experience of the sacred. Panikkar's words describe an aspirational rather than actual aspect of many institutions, religious and otherwise.

WHAT IS SPIRITUAL PRACTICE?

In all world religions, some aspect of community forms in which religious rituals and ceremonies may be performed. These rituals and ceremonies differ in part from spiritual practices in that they are meant to be efficacious or to "work" for an individual or community given the thought system that underlies these performances. They can, however, form a person's being in ways that spiritual practice, too, is meant to. Spiritual practices are those activities a person undertakes in order to be intentional about being the person they want to be or understand themselves to really be—apart from other people's expectations of them—and to employ the virtues or values they most want to practice embodying for themselves, their families, and their friends in relation to an ultimate value of some kind, and in relation to the world as it manifests in local bioregions and in the universe more widely. This sounds far-ranging, in terms of describing a large assortment of activities, and indeed, spiritual practices can be anything that contributes to the formation of a person's being and the sustenance of that person's well-being. Discerning whether or not something is spiritual practice is a matter of personal and communal adjudication, as flourishing is honestly appraised by an individual in relation to their own needs and those of a community. For instance, for one person, ample periods of solitude might be essential to their well-being; for another person, an activity that draws more on their bodily exercise in the natural world, with other people and animals, might constitute what they need for the maintenance of their well-being. The word "practice" in this context is meant to align with other forms of practice, such as practicing a sport or musical instrument. Such activity *changes* us as we are intentional about undergoing the work. We do not necessarily have a goal, such as becoming the perfect soccer player or pianist, but we do understand ourselves to be changing into people more capable of relating with a soccer ball or piano alone or with others. Just so does spiritual practice enable us to grow into the selves we imagine ourselves capable of being and are encouraged to be, growing from the seeds implanted in us from our earliest childhoods as our temperaments and personalities form, our unique gifts and abilities emerge, and our preferences and comfort levels with certain kinds of activities solidify. Increasingly, as we engage spiritual practices of all kinds, we become people able to respond with compassion to whatever disturbances or distresses we come up against, having spent enough time learning to become more aware of ourselves, accept ourselves, and appreciate ourselves.

APPROACHES TO GREENING SPIRITUAL PRACTICES

A greater desire for authenticity and coherence in a person's life also informs the actions of adherents to these world wisdom traditions to green their spiritual practices. To live in such a way as to not experience oneself as disjointed by joining, for instance, in religious rituals that have no bearing on the choices one makes at the supermarket or one's workplace, and vice versa, has arisen as a priority for many in faith communities. Starting from existing spiritual practices and revising them in ways that feel significant for life in the world today, this approach to greening spiritual practice confirms the importance of practice itself as a component of a vibrant life of faith while requiring that age-old practices change to fit life in a world that is increasingly compromised in its integrity through human actions.

This approach of revision is a middle-of-the-road approach to engagement of spiritual practice in the context of contemporary ecological crisis. It differs from approaches that emphasize innovation, which will be discussed in the next chapter, and recovery. An approach that emphasizes recovery posits enough eco-friendly value in the practices or worldviews of a tradition as is, without need for change. This mode recovers eco-friendly aspects of typical practices in existing world religions that may not have sufficiently fed the body of believers but might do so if "recovered" and put into practice; this mode of recovery might also listen for the values expressed in Indigenous traditions that have been silenced by dominant world religions.

The mode of innovation might radically alter existing practices so that they bear very little resemblance to what appears in existing world religions, but innovation also works at the edge of religious identity, often positing very little or no value in traditional practices and thus moving innovators away from religious traditions and their practices in order to create beyond religious communities, though their innovative work often remains useful and transformative for those in religious communities as well and might even build from prototypical elements common within human experience across religious traditions.

The innovation and recovery approaches emphasized in this chapter affirm that while there is value in traditional practices, there is even more value in them when revised in a manner that takes seriously our context of ecological crisis and our need to recover a sense of ourselves as belonging within the world. Specific practices in world religions give us a taste of what is involved in doing this work of revising or greening so that if we are members of a faith community, we may be given ideas for how to do our own work of greening other practices. If we are not members of a faith community, we may at least recognize what work can be done in those communities to effect change, and we might even support that work.

Darshan (a Hindu spiritual practice), an ecological examen (a Christian spiritual practice), eco-halal and eco-kosher dietary practices (Islamic and Jewish spiritual practices, respectively), the metta meditation (a Buddhist spiritual practice), and the Sabbath (a Jewish and Christian spiritual practice) are examples of greening spiritual practice that enable us to see how different traditions have made revisions and extensions to these practices that help adherents of the traditions respond meaningfully to their own needs to flourish and be part of a flourishing ecosystem. Some practices involve the body explicitly, such as choices of food consumed, while others involve use of the mind and exercise of the spirit. Bringing these together underscores the holistic nature of ecospiritual renderings of traditional practices. No aspect of our lives is separate from engagement with the sacred in the natural world, and no routine or habit of our lives cannot be greened so that it could become an ecospiritual practice.

These examples of ecospiritual practice give us a good prism for looking at engagements within and beyond faith traditions, and any person may feel invited to participate in these practices without affirming all of the belief systems that cohere with these traditions. The work of greening spiritual practices renders them accessible to many who might want to change the way they do things in the world in order to become more active in the work of repairing or healing the Earth, a process reflected in the Jewish phrase *tikkun olam* (repair of the world). While the greening of the practices in this chapter may feel most relevant to those who already practice a less green version of them, they are also presented as invitations to consider further greening work to be done in these traditions and as invitations to consider the ethical implications involved in engaging these practices as relevant more widely.

DARSHAN:
THE SACRED ART OF BEHOLDING

A friend once described to me her experience of being in India as revealing to her the ubiquity of the divine. She felt that everywhere she went, she passed shrines devoted to deities, and this was new to her and a contrast to her own tendency, matured in the United States, of locating God or the divine in churches managed by priests. These shrines in India were available everywhere and enabled worshippers to readily act on their intention to show love and reverence to divine beings important in and generative of Hindu spiritual life. The visibility of the sacred was obvious in India in a way not so in the United States, according to my friend.

Another important aspect of Hindu spiritual life is the life in community, especially the life of discipline or asceticism that is shared in ashrams or dedicated spaces for living an intentional spiritual life and embodying the lessons received from a spiritual teacher. Even outside the ashram, however, people have special relationships with teachers or gurus who teach them in various ways and lead them in worship. The practice of *darshan*—meaning seeing or being seen by the sacred—enables a person to affirm the value, and indeed the sanctity, of their guru through beholding in a deeply contemplative manner. Such practice affirms the saying that actions speak louder than words, for just beholding one's guru meditating or praying as one is led within one's own meditation or prayer practice can be more transformative than just hearing the instructions "do this or do that."

Darshan is often practiced in processions when a guru or Hindu saint is not present, but their image (or *murti*) is carried reverently, allowing followers to regard the image as a kind of substitute for the presence of the guru or saint and to respond to the image with the reverence and love a wise and compassionate guide evokes. These ways of practicing darshan are ancient and integrated into people's spiritual lives because of their deeply transformative and efficacious possibilities. To display one's respect and reverence for a particular person whom one regards as divine in a habitual or practiced manner leads to an ability to sense and appreciate divinity in others.

A person who has made her own revision to or expansion of this practice is a woman named Amma, known popularly as the hugging saint, who allows her followers to perform darshan in a radically embodied manner involving physical contact. She gives her followers hugs, and indeed, many people outside the Hindu religious tradition have enjoyed her hugs, which are a radically generous form of offering of the self from a religious leader—quite distinct from teachings received from a pulpit for a listener's edification or spiritual transformation.[2] Just think of it! Just think of being in an assembly of thousands of people all hopeful to receive a hug from a woman whose most important intention is to make you realize the reality of your own being beloved and to communicate that in her own embodiment of divinity in the act of embrace. This is experiential learning at its best! For some, such intimacy could be problematic and in certain contexts taken advantage of. However, it is not uncommon for many people in modern, developed countries to live either alone or even with others and to go a long while without human contact. Such deprivation affects us in ways we likely do not yet fully understand.

The best representation of greening darshan practice is by Shephali Patel, a farmer and educator in New York whose Hindu background informs her making her work with land and people one of spiritual practice. She claims that nature is her temple.[3] She describes the practice of darshan as "seeing the divine in an image, a person, place, or a set of ideas."[4] Practicing darshan means bearing witness to this divinity in the other. And although many from other traditions might fear lapsing into idolatry when considering the divinity of another, Patel makes clear that this practice arises from a sensibility devoted to consideration of everything as sacred. Certainly, the act of beholding in this manner changes how one acts in relation to others, who are considered sacred. Greater care, respect, and reverence become possible and even mandatory. It would be impossible to desecrate (note the word!) something one understands to be sacred. The fact that so much of our environment is in fact desecrated arises from the abandonment of consideration of this part of our world as sacred.

Patel offers a compelling view of darshan as a practice that initiates a person into a reciprocal relationship with the other so that one is not just objectifying the other and reducing them to subjection by one's own gaze. Rather, Patel describes that in the practice of darshan, "you bear witness to something that is gazing back at you."[5] This startling realization comes as one's own subjectivity is ushered into relationship with another subjectivity, be that an animal's or tree's, mountain's or river's subjectivity. Indeed, one is further issued into a new set of virtues and dispositions when in relationship with a reciprocal activity of bearing witness and being witnessed. Two such dispositions might be humility and empowerment. We recognize that others have a life quite beyond our own designs and understanding; further, we grow in our sensitivity as we recognize the limits of our knowledge. This is transformative practice and enables us to dwell in the reality that every place we encounter and every being within it has a life being lived, that we are a part of that life, and that our actions may impact that other life in good and bad ways. Our ability to recognize and regulate our impact on other beings in our ecosystems and bioregions is an amazing gift and responsibility, drawing on our abilities to imagine and to empathize, to which we achieve greater access as we spend time contemplatively engaging others as divine.

Patel does not often write about worship—an activity typically characterizing relationships with the divine—so much as she underscores the love that manifests as we practice darshan as recognition of the divinity of the other. The same love and care a person might feel for a god or goddess springs ultimately from the fact that that being has power, especially generative power, and perhaps of creation itself. We would not exist at all but for the generosity of divine powers. This association of creation and generation and fecundity with the divine naturally maps onto women who are mothers or are capable of being mothers, and the divine feminine probably thrives best in Hindu culture because this association is so readily accepted and understood. Without bypassing the relationship between the divine and the feminine human, we can also recognize how the environment provides everything we need—and that our being originates, most fundamentally, in the bodies of our human parents and then with every aspect of our life that is embedded within the context of our ecosystems and utterly reliant on them. Even the word "embedded" still unfortunately implies dissociation, as if something alien, like a rock, were stuck in the mud of the natural world. Rather, we are that natural world, and our recognition of our interconnectedness with all that surrounds us allows us to quite easily develop attitudes of gratitude, care, love, reverence, respect, praise, celebration, and perhaps even adoration of all that shares our natural home.

Greening the practice of darshan then has the potential to reconfigure our relationships with others, both human and more-than-human, as we recognize and pay homage to the divinity that manifests in and as each other. Avoiding the pitfall of ingratiating subservience to the other and seeing them as so much better than ourselves—reifying the hierarchies we need yet to transform—we recognize our own divinity as well and our own potential for acting as benevolent, loving cocreators and caretakers in this world we share with so many others.

ECOLOGICAL EXAMEN:
THE SACRED ART OF DISCERNMENT

In the Catholic Ignatian tradition, the daily practice of the examen, or examination of conscience, is extremely important. During this practice, one spends time in deliberation while recalling when one has sensed the divine during the day and when one has not. Ignatian tradition talks about these experiences as consolation (recognizing God in all things) or desolation (failing to recognize God in all things). These recognitions manifest as feelings or emotions; that is, one feels consolation as happiness or satisfaction, and one feels desolation as sadness or depression. Though many may intellectually know or affirm that God's presence is a given fact, our experience of this knowledge varies considerably, and we can pay attention to this experience when we notice how our whole selves register feelings of presence or absence.

The meaning of the examen practice involves growth in one's self-understanding and in recognizing what prevents one from beholding God in *all* things. It might be easy to feel grateful to somebody, or Somebody, for the good things that happen during our days, like a good meal or catching up with a good friend. To understand God or

the circumstances of our world—like food production and relationships in community—as the reasons it is possible to enjoy a good
meal or have a conversation with a friend is an understanding we
might aspire to or that might come easily to us. On the other hand,
when bad things happen, like illness or accidents, we can be hard
pressed to consider how God remains a part of our experience. Or if
God is understood to remain a part of it, we may automatically think
"He" is angry with us or that we deserved something bad to happen
to us. We have so much talent for inventing stories to make sense out
of things that can, ultimately, not make any sense at all.

There are many resources that represent the Ignatian examen in
various forms as a practice of self-reflection and prayer. It can be done
midday to reflect on one's morning and at the end of the day to look
back over the whole day. The examen is an excellent tool to train
oneself to be mindful not only during these periods of reflection but
also in the intervening time between exercise of the examen in order
to heighten one's awareness of what is happening during one's day to
promote or obscure awareness of God's presence.

Typically, the practice involves five steps: to be intentional about
being aware of God's presence, to experience gratitude for one's day,
to register what emotions one feels, to recall an incident during the
day that evokes further self-reflection and engage God directly around
the memories of that incident, and finally, to ready oneself for moving on to the remainder of the day or into the next day. This practice
cultivates the kind of gentle compassion we might readily extend to
others but more rarely feel entitled to offer to ourselves. If an incident
in our day makes us feel miserable or joyful, the examen gives us
time to acknowledge those feelings, recognize their temporary nature,
admit failings or ways in which we might want to further grow, and
to let loose the hold that negative emotions might try to keep on
us as we recognize that another day will bring fresh opportunities.
The liberating movement that this practice invites the practitioner
to is something many of us need, preferable to forever carrying along
with us the burdens of past mistakes and the inability to forgive ourselves for them. This of course applies to people of faith as much as

it does to climate activists or others concerned about implementing eco-action in ways that might or might not fulfill their own expectations of themselves. The examen cultivates not complacency around one's failures but rather a readiness to let go of the energy involved in holding onto guilt feelings in order to move more effortlessly into renewed commitment and meaningful action.

The examen practice is readily greened when we begin to translate our question of whether we have beheld God in all things and widen the range of possibilities meant by the words "God" and "all things." We might also ask questions about how we recognized—or did not recognize—the sacred in the natural world. When did we act in ways that were harmful to the natural world or animals or plants? How might we acknowledge this harm and resolve to act in better ways tomorrow? Might these questions make change more readily possible for those of us earnest to do our best but often making mistakes, enabling us to avoid feeling the paralysis that can arise when we focus on the wrongs we do and feel bound to make the same mistakes again and again? Quite appropriately, the Eco-Jesuit website provides instructions that help us see how this self-examination practice from hundreds of years ago has been revised to meet our own and our century's pressing needs. With these instructions, we find the stages developed by Ignatius of Loyola to extend to consideration of how we have interacted with creation:

> Gratitude: I give thanks to God for creation and for being wonderfully made. *Where did I feel God's presence in creation today?*
>
> Awareness: I ask for the grace to see creation as God does— in all its splendor and suffering. *Do I see the beauty of creation and hear the cries of the earth and the poor?*
>
> Understanding: I ask for the grace to look closely to see how my life choices impact creation and the poor and vulnerable. *What challenges or joys do I experience as I recall my care for creation? How can I turn away from a throwaway culture and instead stand in solidarity with creation and the poor?*

Conversion: I ask for the grace of conversion towards ecological justice and reconciliation. *Where have I fallen
short in caring for creation and my brothers and sisters?
How do I ask for a conversion of heart?*

Reconciliation: I ask for the grace to reconcile my relationship with God, creation, and humanity, and to stand
in solidarity through my actions. *How can I repair my
relationship with creation and make choices consistent with
my desire for reconciliation with creation?*[6]

Just as the traditional examen has helped centuries of Jesuits,
Jesuit-educated Catholics, and others gain deeper self-awareness and
deeper relationship with God, so the greening of this particular spiritual practice in the context of the twenty-first century deepens a
practitioner's awareness of God in their care for creation and facilitates the transformation of the practitioner's intention to be more
deliberate in their care of creation. Greening of the examen retains
the framework of the practice while revising its contents only slightly
so that they include activities that affect members of the practitioners'
worlds, human and other-than-human. Experiencing the ongoing
"conversion" dimension of Ignatian spirituality means we accept the
scientific and spiritual overtones of that word as it refers to substances
that change. A regular word in religious contexts to indicate changes
of an interior disposition, "conversion" nevertheless manifests in outward, observable behaviors, which facilitate substantial change. The
two work together: changes in actions that inform our best ideas and
understanding of ourselves and our lives in this world and changes in
our ideas that inform our actions.

ECO-HALAL AND ECO-KOSHER: THE SACRED ART OF EATING

Food has a significant role in the life of a faith community, whether for
Christians when they partake of the eucharistic meal or for Muslims

when they share a festive meal to break the day of fasting during Ramadan. The food one chooses to eat in everyday life also has an impact on one's spiritual life. Of course, awareness of the cruelties of factory farming and its harmful effects on the environment has led some to vegetarianism or veganism. Consideration of these dietary choices as ecospiritual practice is a fruitful endeavor, as vegetarians and vegans often think of their choices as contributing to their own and others' well-being. Religious traditions also propose frameworks that are ethically based for the decisions their adherents will make about food. Both Islam and Judaism, for instance, are traditions that draw from sacred Scriptures and the laws in those Scriptures to determine what foods should or should not be eaten. Compassion seems to be the common link for contemporary practice in these traditions of treating animals who will be consumed well, and some of this compassion continues even after the death of the animal, such as in keeping even the milk of a mother animal separate from the meat of the animal's offspring (Exod 23:19).

In Islamic traditions, Ramadan is a season observed annually when fasting occurs between sunrise and sunset. The person who fasts tempers their own bodily experience of food within these diurnal movements of dawn and dusk. This alone makes this practice quite significant in that very few practices are so explicit in their framing as to acknowledge the ways in which another natural element *governs* one's behavior—the sun, in this case. However, the way one breaks one's fast in the evening requires careful attention and is usually experienced within community as a festive meal. That a sacred fast be broken ethically—with foods that have been obtained with compassionate treatment of animals whose bodies are eaten and with wages that justly reflect the work of the ones who tended the animals or plants or made the foods—is essential for underscoring the sacred quality of the time spent fasting and of the festive breaking of the fast with family and friends. Eco-halal is a designation that serves as an endorsement not only that meat is halal, meaning an animal has been killed compassionately, but that the animal has also been raised in the context of responsible and environmentally friendly behaviors on the part of the farmer or other persons involved in food production services.

Similarly, within Judaism the term *eco-kosher* describes a way of greening one's life more broadly than just that involving dietary customs. Rabbi Arthur Waskow believes that keeping food regulations as stipulated in the Jewish Torah may have appropriately enabled one's right relationship with Earth in the past. Though biblical scholars vary in their interpretations of why some foods are allowed to be eaten and others are forbidden, in keeping kosher, the Jewish people were attentive to the ways that food assisted them in keeping their broad covenants with God, each other and other peoples, animals, and the land. In the twenty-first century, our relationship with Earth is still largely mediated through food. But other areas of concern to people like Rabbi Waskow involve energy use and money.[7] To elaborate this fuller sensibility or greening of the keeping of Jewish kosher laws, we might ask, "Are tomatoes that have been grown by drenching the earth in pesticides 'eco-kosher' . . . Is newsprint that has been made by chopping down an ancient and irreplaceable forest 'eco-kosher' to use for a newspaper? Are windows and doors so carelessly built that the warm air flows out through them and the furnace keeps burning all night 'eco-kosher' for a home or a public building? Is a bank that invests the depositors' money in an oil company that befouls the ocean an 'eco-kosher' place to deposit money?"[8] This greening of kosher practice espoused by Waskow and others means that the term *kosher* itself—so important for observant Jews—comes to act as a signifier for the right relationships that the Jewish covenants were meant to perform. This example in particular provides a sense in which religious legislation may be reinvigorated and given greater significance and import in a time of ecological crisis in its greening by followers who desire to live by such legislation. For Christians, a resonating example might involve greening the Beatitudes from Jesus's Sermon on the Mount, which Steven Chase does in his book *Nature as Spiritual Practice*.[9] Such examples invite other people of faith to investigate their own sacred proscriptions of certain behaviors to discern in what ways they might be greened to attend to the exigencies of our own time. Ecologically conscious Muslims and Jews have set a good example in their practices of eco-halal and eco-kosher for others to reflect more broadly on their commitments to environmentally responsible behaviors.

METTA MEDITATION: THE SACRED ART OF COMPASSION

Compassion, or loving-kindness, does not come easily for all. It often requires intentional cultivation if we want to become more compassionate people. The world today needs compassionate people. More importantly, the world needs people who recognize that their pain for what is happening in the world does not prohibit action on behalf of those most suffering. The world needs people able to feel their own pain that springs from compassion and to enable that to fund their actions. Buddhist tradition has a lively practice of meditation that involves the cultivation of compassion. It goes back many centuries to a sutra on loving-kindness, and instructions have grown up over the centuries over how to carry out this particular meditative practice, involving the use of words that function as a mantra rather than, as is typical in Zen Buddhist meditation, the emptying of one's mind of all words and thoughts. Drawing from other Buddhist traditions, metta meditation resonates with other traditions' practices of intercessory prayer and benediction. The practice, because it allows one to speak an intention on behalf of others, becomes the occasion for making real the feelings of compassion that are expressed aloud by one's voice or inwardly in one's mind.

In a way, the practice is a kind of "fake it until you make it" practice because we may start it with absolutely no compassion for some of the people the traditional form asks us to consider. Nevertheless, this aspect of any spiritual practice is very important and functions not only to manifest what might remain latent in us otherwise but also to make real what may not yet be realized. In many other kinds of practice, the "fake it until you make it" approach is essential to getting over the initial feeling that one is unworthy, incapable, or an imposter—all quite typical experiences of even the most capable of us.

For the metta meditation practice, practitioners choose statements of blessing for others that begin with "may . . ." and often include wishes for happiness, good health, satisfaction, well-being, lack of suffering, and peace. While specific ways these statements are expressed vary, they all involve some dimension of wishing for positive experiences for others as well as the cessation of negative experiences another might have. Phrases that I find useful are the following:

May _____ be happy.
May _____ be at ease.
May _____ not suffer.
May _____ dwell in peace.

Metta meditation involves the repetition of these phrases for four or five different categories of people that might be the same people every time you engage the practice or might change over time, as a really difficult person to get along with might become a neutral person over time. The point of the practice is to draw on the natural warmth, goodness, and intelligence we all have in order to wish the best for others. This natural warmth, goodness, and intelligence may seem hard to access initially, but Buddhists and others believe that it is there and emerges with repetition of the blessings over time.

The first round of using these phrases expresses the wish that you yourself experience these things. Thus, "May I be happy . . ." This can, for some, be extremely difficult to do if we have histories of low self-esteem or trauma that make us feel we do not deserve such experiences as being happy, being at ease, not suffering, or dwelling in peace. It may then be important for some of us to take a long while on this particular part of the practice and to be transformed by an increasing comfort level with being able to wish this for oneself rather than to move on quickly to wishing the best for others.

For those able to move on, the second round involves wishing that another for whom it is very easy to wish these experiences takes the place of "I" in the sayings: "May my partner (or mother or child or best friend) be happy . . ." Traditional Buddhist language uses "benefactor" for this round to speak of someone to whom one owes a great deal and for whom it would thus be easy to slip into language of wishing well in return. Another round might involve someone dear to us, and I usually combine these two rounds. But if it is helpful to distinguish them and to wish well two different people in your experience, go for it. The next round involves someone neutral to us, and this can be a powerful experience as we train ourselves to be attentive to people whose activities we are perhaps indifferent to or whom we would not otherwise notice: someone we randomly see walking in our neighborhood or pass in the supermarket, the person who delivers our mail, or someone at school or work whom we do not know well. "May that person be happy . . ."

Finally, for many, the most difficult round is to pick someone whom you dislike or with whom you do not readily get along. Traditional language speaks of this person as an "enemy," but you may not readily identify many people in your life as enemies. Rather, think of someone with whom you may have had a conflict lately. Is it possible to wish that this person be happy? Be at ease? Not suffer? Dwell in peace? Sometimes, it is not possible, especially if the conflict is really fresh. In addition, if you have experienced significant trauma or abuse because of this person, it may not be healthy for your psychological well-being to think much about wishing them well yet or to move beyond the wound that still needs healing attention in other ways than the metta practice. For some, it is useful to think of aspects of themselves they dislike or have not fully accepted and to wish that part of themselves well. Thus a few examples of how to use this part of the practice that might be difficult, but not as difficult as engaging a person who has seriously hurt you, might be "May that person who just cut me off in traffic be happy . . ." or "May my neighbor who plays loud music late at night be happy . . ." or "May the part of myself that worries so much be happy . . ."

This practice as it stands could effect large-scale transformation if all people were able to identify their real needs and unmet needs and to understand when they try to meet needs in ways that do not truly meet them but rather result in suffering. Such transformation would come, as well, as people accepted that others do this, just the same as they do, and compassion might become the measure of our interactions, large and small. The greening of this practice, however, involves including other categories of beings beyond the human. Could we, as we become proficient in wishing ourselves and our human neighbors well, also wish well our other creaturely neighbors? "May all migrating birds be happy . . ." or "May the trees in the neighborhood park be happy . . ." or "May the ocean be happy . . ." Does it feel awkward to voice these petitions or express these hopes? Does it seem insufficient, as if wishing is not doing and thus inadequate? It seems so important that we do, nevertheless. There is a component of happiness and well-being that all parts of creation need to experience, and it is often in our power to make that possible. We need to want it to happen in order to be intentional about creating the possibilities for it for other life-forms and to be intentional about stopping the behaviors that cause unhappiness and suffering for other neighbors in our Earth community. This practice awakens our heart to necessary actions and cultivates the will to do those actions.

GREENING THE SABBATH: THE SACRED ART OF RECREATION

The first book of the Bible explains a justification for enjoying rest on the seventh day of the week—because God did it. This divine exemplar models behavior that Jews adopt in their own religious or secular contexts. Christians, too, continued the practice, though they moved their experience of Sabbath to what they called "the Lord's day" or the day of Jesus's resurrection, reported in the Gospels as having happened on the day following the Jewish Sabbath. For Christians, this eighth day of the week is identical to the first day of a new week, indicating for some early theologians a cyclical nature of time, experienced in the here and now while also anticipating an eventual "eighth day" that would break human history out of this cycle. For Jews, the Sabbath itself is a day of completion, reflecting God's activity of ceasing from work and contemplating the goodness of all that had been created. Because of their weekly observance of the Sabbath, Jews are invited into a habitual gesture of rest and enjoyment, an attitude of regarding all that is as good, an attitude in imitation of God's pleasure.

A meaningful revision or extension of this particular practice is the application of Sabbath to other times of refraining from certain actions. For instance, a technology Sabbath might describe a period of time in which a person refrains from use of technology for their own well-being and that of those with whom they share community. Getting off our devices, as many Jews do when refraining from work of any kind on the Sabbath—even such seemingly effortless work as use of electricity or public transportation systems—evokes reverence not only for frames of mind and spirit made possible by this disengagement but also for allowing other parts of creation to experience their own rest, when not having to work to make our lives more convenient.

How might a person rest from interacting with various things in their life that perhaps sap their energy? How might one use this rest time, also, to grow in awareness of what it is that we may be addicted to or consumed by? For many in industrialized countries, rest is revolutionary. Rest is countercultural. Rest proclaims that our value is not in what we make or do or can buy or sell. Our value lies in who we are. And we may not know or experience that value unless we intentionally take time to not be defined by our actions or products. This can be particularly hard for people whose value has been affirmed for them by their grades, athletic performance, musical ability, artistic gifts, or some other such component of their being that is admired or praised by others. To begin to dissociate one's unconditional acceptance in community from these talents or gifts is an important part of our spiritual development. We can do this in the context of attending more consciously to the needs of our biotic community by refraining from actions that compromise, for instance, marine and other animal habitats, contribute to polluted skies, and have other negative effects on our larger Earth community.

A weekly respite is the traditional observance of the Sabbath. However, moments of reminding oneself that one's worth comes from being and not doing could be interspersed intentionally into every day. Similarly, a designated day every month for catching up— experientially, in the body—on one's knowledge of one's uncondi- tionally accepted being could be useful for most people with some amount of privilege and leisure to have such a day. Even yearly setting aside a day or weekend or series of days when one can get into the long-term habit of living into the reality of being instead of doing is a spiritual practice worth cultivating and an ecospiritual practice when we are intentional too about the context of our practice and effects of our practice on the Earth community.

We have already been introduced to Wendell Berry's practice of keeping Sabbath holy by writing Sabbath poems that explore the fre- quent difficulty of keeping this rest and that exalt the natural world for setting an example for such rest and for operating by another set of values than production and consumption—activities that charac- terize most of our time and that most of us do not cease even when given an opportunity to do so.

A liberationist reading of the commandment in Jewish Scriptures to keep the Sabbath reveals the injustice of our economic systems that rely on people being unemployed to create demand among a workforce, not all of whose members will be paid fairly. Thus rest- ing on the Sabbath after six days of employment may actually sound pretty privileged to many people in our world today, and we should approach our greening of spiritual practices with that caveat in mind. Certainly, part of the reason to green such spiritual practices might be to give attention to social and environmental injustices that are created when we do not green a spiritual practice. As is, the Sabbath, like other spiritual practices, might only facilitate space within a Jew- ish household to ritualize a family meal and express blessings over the food that nourishes the family and the family members who are nour- ished. Wendell Berry greened the Sabbath in his own Christian con- text to reconfigure his work and leisure rhythms and his attending to the wisdom of the natural world's peace. By greening this practice of

Sabbath, we both attend to the powerful dimensions of a communal meal while extending the transformative potential of a meal throughout all dimensions of society. A community where I live in Portland, Oregon, has adopted Sabbath, as well as Jubilee and Shalom, as a core value and practice for their own community's well-being and the change they want to effect more widely. This group, known as the Wilderness Way, writes about how they practice Sabbath, affirming what they are paradoxically "doing" when ceasing from doing on the Sabbath. These activities are as follows:

> Resisting the pressure to incessantly "do" and "produce" by re-grounding oneself in the beauty, abundance and trustworthiness of the sacred universe, in order to:
>
> > Restore balance to self and relationships
> > Remember who we are and why we are here, and
> > Rekindle creativity and passion for life.[10]

Perhaps the best way to "do" these things is to prioritize spending time with loved ones while sharing meals, memories, playtime, and general recreation. That word—recreation—actually is very evocative of what Sabbath is meant to accomplish through our ceasing to do anything ourselves and letting time and the places we inhabit do the work of changing us, of restoring us, of healing us. The Wilderness Way community aims for this personal and communal work to have far-reaching implications as a counternarrative to the capitalistic, imperialistic society we live in that values us according to what we contribute to the gross national product. Further, this countercultural work counters the narrative that teaches us to value ourselves and each other in this way. During Sabbath, a mentality—one we might hope could permeate our other days of the week—emerges that we are valued simply because we are and we value others simply for who they are and not for what they might do for us. We cease to consider others as objects of our own gratification or to instrumentalize them to our own purposes.

CONCLUSION

Each of the instances of greening spiritual practice in this chapter is meant to suggest avenues of creativity for anyone whose identity is already formed by a community of faith and practice. Whether or not your own community was named in this chapter, you now have examples of how greening practices in your own context might be done. Whatever you do already within the auspices of your faith community might indeed already have significant green dimensions that could be celebrated by your community—meaning they are practices already facilitating your own well-being and growth without harming other members of the Earth community and perhaps even more positively benefitting other members of the Earth community. If activities in your community of faith do not seem to have explicit green dimensions, this chapter suggests ways you might begin rethinking the significance of your commitments.

The five practices in this chapter have each emphasized a different part of our whole lives and the activities we pursue in those arenas of our lives that could be greened in significant ways. In sequence in this chapter, they represent the multileveled aspects of our experience. Darshan emphasizes the importance of beholding with reverence, of being in a relationship with another that expresses the intrinsic value of the other, and of experiencing, as well, reciprocity in knowing oneself to be beloved. This practice affirms the relationality experienced between oneself and others, the spiritual guide and the natural world. The ecological examen invites us to go deeply into our daily experience, recalling feelings of abundance and emptiness and emphasizing the transformative power of asking oneself questions and taking the time to regularly check in with oneself about one's growing ability to discern where and when the sacred is especially present to one and when one's awareness of that presence is obscured by other things. Eco-halal and eco-kosher practices expand our consideration of ethical engagement with one's sources of energy, beyond that of food, both in one's own personal choices and in the choices one makes as a member of a community brought together to share food or other things sourced by energies that we must take care of. Metta meditation trains our hearts and minds to respond to the plight of the natural world with compassion, even those parts of it and ourselves that may feel threatening to us at this time. Finally, the Sabbath invites us to shape our time and use of resources in ways that are more friendly to the Earth community of which we form a part.

Questions for Reflection and Discussion

- What feels familiar or strange about the practice of darshan? Are there people in your life who minister to you just by virtue of existing and whom you behold with pleasure?
- Reflect on the movements of the examen. Regardless of your religious identity, is there a movement that you feel would satisfy a need you have for growing your self-awareness?
- How might eco-halal and eco-kosher movements model an attention to food and consumer practices, especially with regard to energy sources, that you might also experiment with?
- If you were to practice metta meditation, for whom would you feel drawn to express compassion? To whom does your heart reach out?
- How might you incorporate a meaningful period of rest into your day, week, month, or year? How does it feel to contemplate doing such a thing?

Suggested Ecospiritual Practices

Pick one of the ecospiritual practices described in this chapter and tailor it to your circumstances. Could you, for instance, spend some time beholding a beloved place and regarding it lovingly as a guru? Could you adopt the framework of the ecological examen to spend some time at the end of the day deliberately discerning in what ways you habitually contribute to the well-being of the world and expressing your regret for areas where you may have failed and resolve to do better in the new day? Could you examine your food sources, and your other vital necessities, to determine whether they are humanely procured, and could you make changes as you find places to do so? Could you set aside time to cultivate compassion for yourself and others? Could you designate time in a day or week or month to act as "Sabbath," in which you celebrate your being and not your doing? Consider this an invitation to engage a spiritual practice that has already been greened in a significant way and, further, to experiment with your own greening of spiritual practices you might already engage.

Second, do not necessarily pursue this revision of your own commitments in isolation, but use the opportunity to reflect with good friends, family members, neighbors, coworkers, or members of your faith community about how what seem like ordinary commitments might achieve new relevance and significance in this time of planetary crisis and change. Find common ground even with members of other faith or social communities and see where your values and commitments overlap in order to enhance dialogue, exchange, and solidarity. You might volunteer with an organization that plants trees or picks up garbage, cares for animals or works to change energy policy, and engage other volunteers on how they consider their work a component of their spiritual lives—lived oriented to affirming, caring for, and celebrating the sacred earth. Consider this an invitation to deepen the impact and significance of interreligious dialogue and understanding through interspiritual and ecospiritual practice.

For Further Reading

Green Buddhism: Practice and Compassionate Action in Uncertain Times by Stephanie Kaza (Shambhala, 2019)
Green Deen: What Islam Teaches about Protecting the Planet by Ibrahim Abdul-Matin (Berrett-Koehler, 2010)

Sabbath: Finding Rest, Renewal, and Delight in Our Busy Lives by Wayne Muller (Bantam, 2000)

Spiritual Ecology: The Cry of the Earth by Llewellyn Vaughan-Lee (Golden Sufi Center, 2016)

This Sacred Earth: Religion, Nature, Environment by Roger S. Gottlieb (Routledge, 2004)

CHAPTER SIX

Innovations in Ecospiritual Practice

> Spirituality is a mode of being in which not only the divine and the human commune with each other but through which we discover ourselves in the universe and the universe discovers itself in us.
> —Thomas Berry, *The Sacred Universe: Earth, Spirituality, and Religion in the Twenty-First Century*

Just as greening spiritual practice requires imagination and thinking outside the box of traditional expressions of religious ritual and ceremony and devotional engagement with sacred texts and concepts, so do innovations occurring outside such traditions. Deep ecology as a self-understanding of humanity as thoroughly a part of our natural world requires that we implement our special gifts as humans, such as self-reflection, imagination, and empathy, to respond to the ways the natural world offers us lessons in how to be human. One thinker especially important in applying the insights of biomimicry to human change and social transformation is adrienne maree brown.[1] Biomimicry refers to design details drawn from the natural world. Engineers use principles discerned from patterns in the natural world to streamline aerodynamics and to improve forms of human transportation and habitation. Though this might be a novel adaptation within scientific modeling, our growth as human beings within our spiritual dimensions has always drawn from examples in our neighbors' emergent and changing lives, as evidenced by numerous examples in sacred scriptures. One example is the opening of the book of Psalms with its evocation of the tree flourishing beside an ample water source to indicate human flourishing when devotionally and regularly connected with the word of God mediated through law. Another example comes from the Tao Te Ching and its evocation of how water gently and powerfully shapes all that it comes into contact with as an indication of how nonforceful action can be just as if not more transformative in human behavior than force. The energies implicated in nonforceful action are routinely employed in physical action (such as in the martial arts) and in interior movements (as in nonviolent communication within oneself and with others).

adrienne maree brown's work engages biomimicry strategies in order to discern in what ways animal and plant populations work together as species to offer lessons to her human readers about their own potential. Certainly, this requires perceptive awareness of the natural world and imagination to apply what we see to what we do ourselves and to who we are. This is actually an ancient technique, as we might recall the fourth-century desert Christian who spoke about the seed in sand that might not grow if tromped all over and who recommended withdrawing from the busyness of our lives in order to let what is in us grow. This is an insight this desert Christian drew from their observation of the natural world, and this person discerned a likeness between themselves and the seed in relationship with the land. This is precisely what adrienne maree brown is doing too as she points out particular natural processes as emergent—that is, they change and can change in large ways because of smaller interactions or smaller components of the whole that create large shifts. The relationship between the small and big gets its fullest attention with brown's focus on emergence.

A few examples may suffice to give us an impression of what brown helps us understand. She writes about how certain birds fly together, altering their collective movement by a subtle signaling between individual members of the flock and modeling emergent, nonhierarchical relationships as no individual bird is in the lead. She writes of mycelium who form an underground network of communication and support, modeling relational interdependence within the species and across species. She writes of the wave-particle duality that resists either/or identity and instead models hybridity and a both/and reality new and challenging to human consciousness. Some thinkers have also used this example from our new knowledge of quantum reality to explain other forms of intelligent movement beyond the human that we signal we do not yet understand by labelling random.[2] In these examples drawn from the natural world, brown suggests that the emergent qualities of human communities, as well, arise from individual, small-level interactions that enable movements on a larger scale. The whole is larger or more significant, then, than the sum of its parts. Other principles that she draws from her minute attention to the natural world and the forms it offers us for imitation include the following:

> Small is good, small is all. (The large is a reflection of the small.)
> Change is constant. (Be like water.)
> There is always enough time for the right work.
> There is a conversation in the room that only these people at this moment can have. Find it.
> Never a failure, always a lesson.
> Trust the People. (If you trust the people, they become trustworthy.)
> Move at the speed of trust. Focus on critical connections more than critical mass—build the resilience by building the relationships.
> Less prep, more presence.
> What you pay attention to grows.[3]

Innovations in ecospiritual practice draw from principles that brown identifies as consistent with emergent strategy. Consideration of zero waste as a spiritual practice, for instance, draws its force from deep investigation of what pollution really means and does. Forest therapy requires that a person slow down and intentionally engage their sensory perception of the sylvan world and regard presence in the forest as therapeutic. The Council of All Beings draws on the imagination and the conviction that there is a creaturely continuity between human and all life on Earth allowing us to live more fully into our identity as members of the Earth community come to consciousness. As Thomas Berry writes, "The Earth is acting in us whenever we act."[4] According to Berry, Earth has even "[taken] a certain amount of control of itself in its human mode of being."[5] This identification of the human species as a form of the universe or Earth come to self-consciousness invites us to new and exciting self-understanding and use of our unique skills to repair the damage we have done on Earth so far.

ZERO WASTE AS ECOSPIRITUAL PRACTICE

Zero waste is a concept used by manufacturers to explain how by-products emerging from the manufacturing process are repurposed to ends that allow them not to be wasted. In the early decades of the twenty-first century, individuals in households have adopted this ideal to frame their own activities of use and repurposing. A principal proponent of this practice is Bea Johnson, a California mother whose book, blog, videos, and appearances to international communities have enabled the practice to be adopted by a wide variety of people all over the world. One reason this practice has emerged and been adopted so quickly is practitioners' use of social media and online community tools to collaborate with one another by sharing ideas and resources. Another reason also draws from online tools: the visibility of waste. Many of us may not live near enough to a landfill to really see, marvel at, or feel concerned about how much waste we routinely deposit there. But others who do have such experiences have shared their experiences online. Further, those who live near unofficial polluted sites have also made these degraded places in nature visible to the rest of us so that we might do something about it.

Among those who have raised awareness of the issue of pollution and its impact on the natural world is the photographer Chris Jordan, whose *Midway* photographs of bird bodies ravaged by plastics and open to disclose their bodies' plastic contents have been profoundly moving to many—urging them to reconsider using a plastic straw or other products that are so easily disposed of and might end up the unappetizing and unnourishing food for creatures elsewhere in the world. Bea Johnson and Chris Jordan are both activists working from their own sources of pain at seeing the natural world so compromised in its integrity, and they are working to evoke others' consciousnesses and compassionate responses to unnecessary uses of plastic and other disposables.

An interesting aspect of this very practical activity of zero waste is its characterization as a spiritual practice. What makes such a practice as recycling or zero waste *spiritual*? To ask this question is to continue thinking of the spiritual as something that refers to something done in religious spaces or for some religious purpose, however we typically define such things. But in our twenty-first-century context, we need to think and act beyond such distinctions and to consider what things we do that contribute to the flourishing of members of the Earth community as *spiritual practice*. In that way, zero waste becomes an important expression of one's spiritual life. It prevents contributing to the problem other parts of creation face when flooded with waste, and it helps us foster alternatives to the kind of "throwaway culture" that we have formed, which extends not only to material objects but also to our relationships and other more intangible aspects of our lives that we may too easily disengage.[6]

Many practitioners of zero waste also reflect on how the practice brings them into community more readily with other activities. Purchasing items without wasteful packaging often means interacting with the producers themselves, such as at a farmers' market or through community-supported agricultural co-ops.[7] Like eco-halal and eco-kosher, this practice impacts so many activities of one's life. Starting with food, we might resist packaging that is disposed of by opting for whole rather than processed foods. This contributes to our bodily health, as well as mediating health to our ecosystems. Another activity, such as the choice of clothing we purchase and wear, might involve thinking about the waste incurred by having to care for and maintain such items and opting for possibilities that will not require wasteful practices of water use or cleaning products. Waste in transportation choices can be eliminated as we make decisions about walking or biking in areas close to us or making one's trips to other places efficient by grouping them in one day.

Scientists affirm the precept that "in nature, nothing is created and nothing is destroyed, but everything is transformed."[8] Nature models an overabundance of resources, and though some aspects of it may seem wasteful, there is a reason, for instance, a fruit tree will produce more blossoms than become fruit. Such abundance expresses the means by which reproduction will occur, and in some ways, our own processes have gotten away from such sensibilities when we focus on scarcity. However, we are invited to be mindful that our natural systems are closed and whatever we throw away goes somewhere and is stored there until it breaks down and is reintegrated into another part of our natural systems. In the case of some substances, this breakdown can take centuries or even millennia. Fortunately, humans are learning from nature how nature disposes of surplus and how everything is fundamentally recycled. What one element of an ecosystem does not need anymore another might use. We can see this balancing out in the simple reciprocal action of respiration that plants and breathing creatures share in: breathing in oxygen that plants provide for us, we then breathe out the carbon dioxide those plants need. Many trees lose leaves seasonally to enter a period of preparation for new growth, and their leaves provide nourishment for soils that feed other inhabitants of a forest, for instance. These models might help us calibrate what forms of waste we tolerate creating in our own lives and what we refrain from creating.

For Christians, the truth of transformation implicit in the practice of zero waste also resonates with resurrection. For Buddhists, a similar resonance may occur between zero waste and reincarnation. Attending to the cycles of renewal that our own bodies experience

in the context of our Earth community trains us to see the nonper-
ishability of aspects of our material culture. Similarly, though often
resurrection or reincarnation may appear as abstractions to us, experienced in ways we do not thoroughly understand, attending as well
to the concrete evidence of the renewal of material culture around
us also has the potential to green and deepen our understanding of
human experience.

FOREST THERAPY: ELIDING SACRED SPACES

In recent years, the transformation of "forest bathing" (shinrin-yoku) in
Japan has been recognized worldwide as forest therapy. Originally,
forest bathing was developed to counter the ennui that accompanied
industrialization and was a social movement to effect a reconnection
between human populations and with the natural world. In more
recent years, forest therapy has emerged as a name for the same activity, and certification programs for becoming a forest therapy guide
have been developed in order to respond to the resurgence of interest
in cultivating a person's sensory experience in the wild as a method
of therapeutic engagement with the natural world. There could be
something a bit troubling about the commodification of the training
process for becoming a certified forest therapy guide, and though I
will not investigate further the ethical components of the market-
ing and consumption of programs like forest therapy certification, I
do mention this aspect of the practice as something warranting further critique. Is it right to pay someone to guide one through a forest therapy session? After all, many people pay for counseling and
other therapeutic interventions. Is it right to pay to become a certified
guide? What does it say about the activity when training in it requires
monetary exchange?

However we answer these questions, the fundamental insight
offered by the transformation of the name "forest bathing" to "forest
therapy" is that it indicates a woundedness on the part of the human

community. Something about human identity has been and is being wounded when not in touch with fundamental aspects of the natural world as sacred. Restoring that connection is understood to lead to a healing of one's woundedness and thus to constitute therapy rather than bathing or cleansing oneself.

An important aspect of forest therapy is that the forest is the therapist, not the person who might guide one through a forest therapy session. The forest setting is primarily responsible for the healing work that occurs when people slow down to engage their senses in the sylvan setting. The guide, certified or otherwise, is trained in leading others to slow down and to use their senses—two activities that might be thought to be natural to us and yet so often are not—and so guides I know are very careful to identify themselves as forest therapy *guides* and not forest therapists themselves, leaving the work of therapy to the forest.

Kimberly Ruffin, a licensed forest therapy guide, writes about the drawing together of the Christian church community and the forest space as holy in her essay "Bodies of Evidence: A Forest Therapy Guide Finds Her Church."[9] In this essay, Ruffin claims, "Faith is the method we use to support the spirit of our human animality," and she says, "Nature is my church, and church is in my nature." Both of these claims help us think beyond the places where we typically locate faith expression and also contest the distinction between the human and our sacred earth home. In an online article, Ruffin also offers guidance to an experience of forest therapy that requires us to pay close attention to the ways our senses apprehend the natural world and locate us in a life-giving relationship of belonging.[10] Notably, though "therapy" has in a sense taken the place of "bathing" in terms of this practice's recognition, the refreshing immersion that bathing suggests can also resonate with what therapy accomplishes for a person.

Much of what occurs during a forest therapy session involves focusing in on key sensory ways of engaging the natural world—by attending to texture and movements that one sees, small or large, or by listening to sounds close to one or farther away and noting the difference. One might sit for a while in one space and allow one's interior noisiness to quiet in response to the subtle and lively noises around one. When therapy is being accomplished, the person begins to experience the reintegrating of their fundamental identity as one member of the Earth community amid many other members. So often, we tend to enter a forest on a trail and purposefully go our way, hiking, but forest therapy is an ecospiritual practice that invites us to resist staying on the trail (though to be safe in our going off-trail, so to speak) and to resist the urge to cover ground quickly. John Muir said, echoing Henry David Thoreau's reflections in his essay on "Walking," "People ought to 'saunter' in the mountains [or forests]—not hike! Do you know the origin of that word saunter? It's a beautiful word. Away back in the middle ages people used to go on pilgrimages to the Holy Land, and when people in the villages through which they passed asked where they were going, they would reply, *A la sainte terre*, 'To the Holy Land.' And so they became known as sainte-terrers or saunterers. Now these mountains [and forests] are our Holy Land, and we ought to saunter through them reverently, not 'hike' through them."[11] We express our experience of the natural world as sacred when we are able to be present regarding all we see and hear, smell and feel, as sacred, as holy land. A friend of mine who is a pastor organizes "Sacred Saunter" experiences for the members of the faith community they serve. Regularly, these members engage the natural world in ways that expand the boundaries of their recognized sacred space, the church building, to comprise the neighborhood parks and woods surrounding that space. As this practice continues, our sensibility concerning the pervasive holiness and sacred quality of all our Earth community will be affirmed and celebrated.

This ecospiritual practice of forest therapy invites us to reconsider where it is we are most nourished and healed. Early Christian theology posited the church or faith community as a site of personal and communal healing and partaking of the eucharistic meal as a medicinal activity that not only might remediate past uncleanliness, in the form of sinful behavior, but could also equip or nourish one for more virtuous activity in subsequent times. When I have experienced forest therapy with a guide, part of the time spent together in a small group has involved eating foods like dried fruits or nuts that come from trees, nibbling on wood sorrel, and drinking tea brewed with pine needles or some other dimension of the particular forest in which therapy was unfolding. For many Christians and other people of faith, this ingestion of a meal together may parallel what they celebrate together in a liturgical setting. It also reminds us of the ways in which we are nourished quite physically, just as we are psychologically and spiritually, by the forest as the forest becomes us and we live out the forest's life in our own bodies. John Muir wrote presciently of this engagement in a letter about "Lord Sequoia," whose blood or wine he consumed sacramentally. He seemed to mean the presence of the trees and mountains and other creatures intoxicated him, and his ecstatic sensibility of transposing going to church to an attitude of responsive fidelity to the forest and mountains that called him can inform our own apprehension of the sacred. "There is balm in these leafy Gileads," Muir claimed. "Sick or successful, come suck Sequoia and be saved."[12] Just as Muir modeled an awareness of the forest's therapeutic nature, so may we become increasingly aware of the larger dimensions of this space that can heal as we spend time in forests. Further, that other sacred spaces like the coastline or prairies or desert also promote healing when engaged to the fullest extent through our sensory experiences renders an openness to those places and ways we can experience healing. That forests offer a privileged place of healing may draw from trees' long-standing association with shrines. The sacred groves of long ago are being again restored in our collective memory as we encounter the diverse communities living in forests and experience the unique respite such spaces offer.

THE COUNCIL OF ALL BEINGS

The Council of All Beings is a ritual developed by Joanna Macy and John Seed to enable participants to experience their own creaturely continuity with other beings and to access the wisdom these other life-forms have for the human community. The Council of All Beings does not draw from any existing ritual, though it uses language of "council" to indicate a gathering of a truly extraordinary kind: that of the human community using imagination to summon the persons of other life-forms and aspects of our universe to speak their experience and even to offer the human community gifts from their experience. While the greening of spiritual practices in the past chapter involved drawing on the wisdom of instructions in sacred scriptures and traditions for how the practice might be activated in one's life, the Council of All Beings draws from a surprising source: a novel by T. H. White published in the late 1950s, *The Once and Future King*. This novel fantasizes about the life of King Arthur and his childhood years before drawing the sword Excalibur from the place where it was lodged in stone, an act that reveals Arthur's identity as future leader of the British Isles. What is so fantastic about this book is how White depicts King Arthur as a child, learning wisdom. Likely drawing on the biblical ascription of paramount wisdom to King Solomon and his own study of natural species (1 Kgs 4:29–34), T. H. White has his fictional child Arthur be mentored by animal species whom he actually becomes through the magic of his friend, the wizard Merlin. Joanna Macy, an ecophilosopher, Buddhist scholar, and one of the creators of the Council of All Beings ritual, describes this background in her own experience from which she drew to create the council: "Knowing that great responsibilities were in store for the boy, the wizard changed him for periods of time into various creatures—a falcon, an ant, a badger, a wild goose, a carp in the castle moat. As we [Macy's family] read each of Arthur's adventures in learning, they stretched our minds and enlarged our perceptions and perspectives beyond what we were accustomed to as humans."[13]

Joanna Macy read this book with her children when they were young, and the idea that one learns best from stepping into the shoes of another, or the paws or wings or another, inspired her to create the Council of All Beings with John Seed. Her later commitment to Buddhist spirituality and to the early tales of the Buddha's lifetimes as animals told in the Jataka tales must have also informed the creation of this ritual.[14] The reading of *The Once and Future King* to inform her approach to this ecospiritual practice is unusual certainly, but it also allows us to think about the sources of our own understanding and practice: fiction might inspire, maternal and family life might inspire. We might be surprised by the places in our own lives that yield some kind of new thinking for creating and reframing ecospiritual practice.

The Council of All Beings is a ritual integrating human ecodespair at the condition of our natural world while also empowering participants to live more fully their embodied dimension of the universe itself. They work from a premise that values "thinking like a mountain," a phrase coined by Aldo Leopold that means valuing the interests of the biotic community, inclusive of the human, rather than the interests of just the human. In fact, the Council of All Beings arose from Macy's work with developing a set of "Despair and Empowerment" rituals that require or invite participants to acknowledge their deep grief at what is happening to our earth home and concurrently empower them to act anew as members enlivened to their identities and to their capacities to live in ways that would not necessarily contribute to the devastation of Earth.

Instructions for the Council of All Being appear in an abbreviated description in Joanna Macy's *World as Lover, World as Self*.[15] Fuller instructions for hosting a retreat or a gathering of individuals to prepare for and enact a ritual of the Council of Beings can be found in *Thinking Life a Mountain: Towards a Council of All Beings* by Joanna Macy with John Seed, Pat Fleming, and Arne Naess.[16] Stages of preparation for the council involve mourning, telling stories and meditating on deep time, and honoring endangered and extinguished species. Then one lets a life-form choose one for representation at the council, one engages one's creativity to make a mask that would allow one to visually represent the life-form at the council that has chosen them, and one speaks for that life-form at the council. The council involves participants taking turns alternately speaking for the life-form that has chosen them and being a human who receives the words of other participants speaking for the life-forms that have chosen them. Here are excerpts from student writing that express identification with life-forms other than human. One student, Meg, writes,

> I live in the dense forests with my family. Most of the day I spend eating to maintain my body mass. My family and I eat all the different parts of plants in our lands, with some occasional bugs. We stay around the same altitude year-round because our food is plentiful there. Life as a mountain gorilla is extremely social. Our family groupings are based on social bonds between male and female adult gorillas. The forests offer us tools for our whole lives, from food to places to sleep at night.
>
> However, life isn't always easy as a mountain gorilla. One problem we face is poaching. People trap smaller animals to sell them on the black market and we'll get caught in the traps, either injured or killed by them. Sometimes our children will be stolen from us and we will be killed in the process. We also face habitat loss. Thankfully, some national parks protect us but as human settlements grow, we lose our lands. We lose contact with other groups of mountain gorillas, reducing the genetic diversity of our groups. To increase conservation efforts, humans come to see us and learn about us. But, they then spread diseases to which we are vulnerable. As humans fight amongst themselves, we lose our homes to people fleeing conflict and we are used as a source of meat for refugees. Slash and burn agriculture also contributes to loss of our habitat and lives.[17]

This writing that expresses the life of a mountain gorilla gets quite detailed in its consideration of the pleasures and pains of gorilla life in contact with humans. A gift the mountain gorilla might offer humans is the gift of social bonds and pleasure in each other's companionship, which humans also know and might revitalize as a way to meet their own needs rather than impact upon or harvest aspects of the mountain gorilla's life. This practice of giving voice to a life-form might remind us of the green lens we explored when engaging the Judeo-Christian Scriptures. Here, we look about the world and pay attention to what draws our compassion and listen for what that life-form has to tell us about ourselves even from the midst of that creature's pain. We already have access to this information, but drawing on our capacities to imagine and empathize, we more readily evoke insights for the work of repairing the world. This practice thus enables participants to rewild their imaginations by considering what life is like from another point of view that, despite being different from a human point of view, taps into some parts of our consciousness able to identify and empathize with other life-forms. Another student, Madison, writes, beginning with a litany of negative human impacts on the life of this creature,

> Dams block my travels. Overfishing prevents my proliferation. Logging erodes the banks of the streams and ruins the shade that keeps them cool. Toxic pollution from pesticides, fertilizer, waste dumping, and boats accumulates in my cells and biomagnifies through the natural beings who consume me. Humans try to help by farming hatchery salmon, but this destroys the resilience of my community more. Genetic variation is key to the survival of any species. When more than half of our population comes from the same hatchery fish, there are fewer mutations in our genome that are required for the adaptations needed to persist through ecosystem disruptions.
>
> Nonetheless, humans can learn from our ways of living to help them make the changes necessary for ours, as well as the entire Earth's, survival. The most notable feature of our lives is our dedication to returning to our roots. The wonder I hold around how I am able to swim to an entirely new place and find my way home through the rapids can be uplifting. Humans should strive to return back to their roots of how to live in touch with nature. Humans once respected and honored nature. That respect and honor has been lost in their current ways of living, but that doesn't mean they can't return to that

same outlook. Even if it means struggling to swim upstream, through whitewater and over waterfalls, it is possible. If I can do it, so can you.[18]

Another student, Macey, writes,

I love my home. I'm able to do as I please, grabbing fish from the rivers to eat as I roam free. There are caves and burrows where I can hibernate, staying warm throughout the winter. I am also a regulator for my ecosystem. By preying on deer and other small woodland creatures I keep their populations from overwhelming the forest. I keep the balance. Lately, things have been different. Daily, light and noise are getting closer to where I like to roam. It's harder to find something to eat. There's less water flowing through the rivers, meaning fewer fish. I'm forced closer to the noise and light. When I walk near human habitation the ground feels different with no grass or dirt. I'm forced to eat plastic and weird-colored food. Humans try to scare me away but I'm so hungry. This food doesn't make me feel good and it's scary when I see humans kill others like me.

Maybe someday humans can respect my boundaries a little more so that I have space to wander in my own home. I don't mind gentle hikers but cars and buildings closer to my home make it harder for me to live a normal life. I hope that humans will become thoughtful. I hope they will make this change so that we can all keep living. I know that they can fix our planet before it's too late.[19]

This third writing ends by anticipating the hope that humans might themselves keep the balance, as bears do within their own ecosystem. We, too, might learn from bears to be good regulators of our habitats and not encroach on other's domains nor overuse the resources available to us where we live.

Writing these tales of creaturely experience offered students ways to package their scientific understanding, often gleaned in environmental studies courses, within a creative form giving expression to the life of a gorilla, salmon, and bear. These wild animals have their own experience of the human, and we learn more about our impact on them when we imagine life from their points of view. We also learn more about ourselves in continuity with these others—we can do the creative work of imagining and empathizing with their experiences when we learn, for instance, as Madison's writing demonstrates, that just as salmon return to "roots" or homeland streams and rivers, so we might return to our own roots. Sharing this metaphor with plant beings reveals how interconnected all our creaturely existence is. We all belong and we all have places to which we particularly belong.

CONCLUSION

Emergent strategy offers us a way to consider our everyday, interpersonal relationships and decisions to be significant because they signal shifts that contribute to the larger-scale movements that are emerging today. The natural world models such emergence every day, and our human tendency to work quickly and become impatient at the rate of change may be tempered when we pay attention to the real ways that natural systems work. A particular reconfiguration of our thinking that might be helpful for us as we experiment and innovate with new practices is to critique our goal of sustainability. Surely, sustainability is a really important goal and one that students studying environmental ethics and policy bring to our class discussions of ecospirituality. One of my teachers helped me question that goal or at least to consider it merely a minimum, as sustainability speaks to how our ways of being might not pillage resources from future generations. However, when we think of relationships in terms of sustainability, we might be disappointed if we think of sustainability as our only goal or ideal. My teacher asked us to consider a human partnership and how we might react if we asked about the relationship and were given the answer, "It's sustainable." That might be good, but it does not reflect likely all the gifts exchanged by those people in a partnership or community. Rather, flourishing may be a better idea to characterize what we want to sustain and work for. Our innovations then in ecospiritual practice must not stop at sustainable behavior but facilitate thriving and flourishing of our own human populations and of other populations we live among.

The work of creating and enacting innovative ecospiritual practices like zero waste, forest therapy, and the Council of All Beings draws on human ingenuity and empathy. Indeed, innovating requires our imaginations to be employed as we thoughtfully regard what life might be like from the perspective of another being. Surely this work has its origins in the social justice movements of our past history and of our present as we gain fuller pictures of what reality is like for another person and from their point of view. We begin to understand the systemic relationships involving power that result in oppression and suffering and to question their legitimacy. The same is true for those whose sympathies for the natural world enable them to apply their imaginative faculties to understanding the plight of an animal or plant living in a compromised, polluted habitat; to imagining the forest as a place where essential healing might happen; and to ritually bringing to voice the perspectives of Earth community members so as to remind humans of their own deepest potential to act with courage and resilience.

Questions for Reflection and Discussion

- How wasteful are you in your everyday life, and how do the ways you treat material objects relate to your treatment of people and relationships, or even of yourself?
- What kinds of landscapes do you find most restorative of your spirit, and why? Think about childhood and where you felt most at home outdoors.
- What or where is "church" to you? If outdoors, what spaces most express the sacred? If indoors, what elements of nature exist there to remind you of your larger sacred home?
- If you were to practice the Council of All Beings, what viewpoint would call to you? How could you begin to express something from that being's perspective?
- What other practical eco-actions do you take in response to the ecological crisis we experience now, and how might those actions be understood as "spiritual"?

Suggested Ecospiritual Practices

Adopt the perspective of an animal or a feature of the natural world that might participate in a Council of All Beings. Do you find that your imagination is a bit creaky or out of practice as you do so? Though practices before this also invited you to use your imagination to honor the perspective of another being, this particular practice enables you to discover new knowledge about yourself. What advice might another creature offer you for living your life in the best manner possible? Further, what actions on behalf of this other creature might suggest themselves to you as a result of this identification? How will you put them into practice? What new knowledge about yourself as a member of the human species do you discover as a result of your ability to "tune in" to this other being's perspective? Do they offer you a gift that, in fact, you already possess, though it is unrecognized and unutilized? To invite accountability, share this exercise or ecospiritual practice with another person, or even a small group. Have some fun with the practice and design masks to wear while you voice the perspective of these animal others or features of the natural world. Fuller guidance and descriptions of past councils can be found in the sources cited in this chapter. Consider this an invitation to play with a part of your human nature that may have been hibernating for too long and be ready to awaken.

One exercise that forest therapy guides offer participants is to look for something in the forest that they understand as something the forest is offering the participant as a gift. As part of a tailored experience of forest therapy alone or with just one or two other people, walk slowly in a forest setting looking at the ground or around you with attentive eyes and a receptive heart open to the gifts of the forest. If you take a leaf or twig with you away from the forest, keep it in a place that reminds you of the giftedness of all the forest offers and plan to return that gift when you are next in that place. This can also be done in other settings, such as on the beach, prairie, or desert. Consider this an invitation to practice respect for a natural place and to share in the pleasure of receiving its gifts while experiencing also the fullness of the cycle of taking and giving by returning the gift, literally and figuratively.

For Further Reading

Becoming Animal: An Earthly Cosmology by David Abram (Vintage, 2011)
Coming Back to Life: The Updated Guide to the Work That Reconnects by Joanna Macy and Molly Brown (New Society, 2014)

Cradle to Cradle: Remaking the Way We Make Things by William
McDonough and Michael Braungart (North Point, 2002)
How Forests Think: Toward an Anthropology beyond the Human
by Eduardo Kohn (University of California Press, 2013)
Undrowned: Black Feminist Lessons from Marine Mammals by
Alexis Pauline Gumbs (AK, 2020)

CHAPTER SEVEN

The Living and Enlivening World

A change is required of us, a healing of the betrayed trust between humans and earth. Caretaking is the utmost spiritual and physical responsibility of our time, and . . . the solution to the mystery of what we are.

—Linda Hogan, *Dwellings:*
A Spiritual History of the Living World

Life-giving principles facilitating Indigenous resurgence and flourishing are coming into global conversation as peoples from differing countries make common cause with unsettling the settler and colonizing cultures and mentalities to which Indigenous peoples have too often and too long been subject. Indigenous resurgence describes a movement in which the dignity of Indigenous peoples, traditions, practices, and spiritualities is recognized and appreciated, both within Indigenous communities and outside them. Many of us who may not consider ourselves tied to Indigenous populations may be beginning to know more about and respect the ways that Indigenous teachings help us reconnect with ourselves and our experience of the natural world—ways that have been lost to many of us. Even some Indigenous peoples, struggling with the impacts of colonization, are retrieving lost parts of their traditions that have been vital to their identities. Recovering and preserving the languages of native peoples is a difficult project when fewer and fewer speakers of these languages survive, and yet the worldviews preserved in these languages are essential to fostering a kinship relationship within the

Earth community, as are the worldviews expressed by many practices of Indigenous peoples.

A concern arising alongside Indigenous resurgence is the appropriation, commodification, and commercialization of Indigenous cultures and spiritualities. These actions continue and exacerbate the work of colonization rather than resist it. Some ways these actions manifest are stereotypes, so we should avoid those when possible. Instead, a deep reverence for the ancient wisdoms that persist in communities that have experienced oppression, silencing, assimilation, and even genocide must be recognized and affirmed in this time of planetary crisis. Further, the word *resurgence* is not meant to indicate that these wisdoms have been lost and recovered necessarily, though in some places and among some communities, these losses may have been suffered and the great difficulty of recovery persists. In other communities, Indigenous custodians of wisdom have been present all long, though perhaps regularly discredited or neglected by those in power. These custodians are now experiencing a surge of recognition and celebration, again both within such Indigenous communities and outside. This chapter aims to honor their work while acknowledging that my own perspective has been formed within a settler culture that profits routinely from past acts of genocide and oppression; my perspective, like many other people's perspectives, is being shaped by attention to the Indigenous peoples in our communities whose work must be affirmed and with whom I express solidarity. As I describe some of the practices emerging from my own context as an educator, I acknowledge my capacity to make mistakes in representation by simplifying or universalizing complex differences among Indigenous peoples of my own country. My work as an educator and here as an author expresses desire to support the leadership of Indigenous peoples in determining what needs to happen to transform past and present injustice and how to do this work.

Among the most influential of recent texts from the perspective of an Indigenous citizen of the United States is Robin Wall Kimmerer's *Braiding Sweetgrass*. As a botanist and member of the Potawatomi Nation, Kimmerer "braids" together three strands of engagement with the natural world: one strand that draws from the legacy of her Indigenous ancestors, one strand from her training as a scientist, and one strand from her listening closely to the plants, ambassadors of the natural world, with whom she works. Kimmerer works with mosses, in particular, and is doing important work to restore wholeness to the field of science and to the perspective and experience of many both inside and outside the sciences. Her work legitimizes this braiding of multiple ways of knowing and of knowledge creation, and global cultures will continue to reap a harvest from her wisdom for years to come. The practices described in this chapter draw from and epitomize the Indigenous resurgence that the popularity of Kimmerer's work represents. Though not meant to trivialize the diversity of many Indigenous communities, these practices provide an entry point into consideration of the value for ecospirituality that the Indigenous resurgence represents. These particular practices facilitate living into the experience of celebrating the living world and the world's enlivening, or life-giving, powers. Practices such as land acknowledgments, the Thanksgiving Address, the Honorable Harvest, and the use of new pronouns for the natural world invite our changed perspective on how the world is animated and animates our own being. Much of what is described here draws on and amplifies the work of Robin Wall Kimmerer.

LAND ACKNOWLEDGMENTS

Among recent developments of Indigenous resurgence are the land acknowledgments shared before gatherings of many kinds. In educational, civic, and religious settings, statements affirming the presence, historical and contemporary, of Indigenous peoples help frame the conversations and activities that happen in that specific place. So many of our public and private spaces these days, across the world, take shape in the usurped spaces of Indigenous peoples. Acknowledging this is a first step to restoration of and reparations to these communities that have, historically and into the present day, experienced marginalization, silencing, and theft of their lands, languages, values, and identities. In the Pacific Northwest where I live, I use a land acknowledgment in my classes at the University of Portland that draws from material that local leaders have provided. It is a statement that acknowledges the names of communities that have been present in this land for millennia. Often these names will sound familiar, having been used as names for streets, parks, or other civic spaces. But when these names are not recognized as the names of Indigenous communities, we can forget how interwoven the histories of Indigenous peoples are with the settler and colonizing peoples newer to this land. The statement adopted by myself and other instructors at the university begins like this, with slight additions in my classes to affirm the continuing presence of Indigenous peoples and their importance in our communities:

> We acknowledge the land which we occupy at the University of Portland: "The Portland Metro area rests on traditional village sites of the Multnomah, Wasco, Cowlitz, Kathlamet, Clackamas, Bands of Chinook, Tualatin, Kalapuya, Molalla, and many other tribes who made their homes along the Columbia River creating communities and summer encampments to harvest and use the plentiful natural resources of the area" (Portland Indian Leaders Roundtable, 2018). As your instructor, I invite you to join me in gratitude for the original and ongoing caretakers of this land and in living in a manner consistent with the respect and reverence due this land and our neighbors, human and other-than-human, with whom we share this land.

This statement appears on course syllabi and is spoken aloud during the first class session. Other places a land acknowledgment is used are community-organized events such as demonstrations, protests, marches, and public meetings. A city council or other governing body would express its members' desire to recognize and affirm the status of stolen lands on which their deliberations ensue if voicing this land acknowledgment before proceedings; further, such members would also be expressing their desire to do something about such stolen status. We do not yet see many civic and judicial spaces that have adopted such a procedure, but this practice is one that can initiate the repair of long-standing grievances and the reintegration into public spaces of people who too often have been left out.

Another place where a land acknowledgment is beginning to be voiced is within faith communities, especially those that have done the work of charting a history of their meeting spaces in order to know how the land upon which churches and other buildings where religious worship takes place came to be owned by certain denominations or individual faith communities. Some communities have a land acknowledgment printed in their worship bulletin, and some make time before a service begins to voice such an acknowledgment. Though not widely adopted yet, this kind of integration of recognition and respect into the practice of a faith community reflects the community's desire to heal the wounds caused by separation of Indigenous peoples from their communities, which was often caused by faith communities removing children to mission schools, for instance. The experience of joining one's expression of faith in community with this recognition—even as it entails grief and lament in recalling the complicity of faith communities, especially Christian, in the wounding of Indigenous communities—can be profound.

As a guide for formulating a land acknowledgment, the website of the Native Governance Center states, "[Land acknowledgments] should function as living celebrations of Indigenous communities."[1] They should empower Indigenous peoples living in the community today and not just memorialize past communities and the struggles these communities may have endured. A land acknowledgment should invite others to reflect on how they have, perhaps unwittingly, been complicit in ongoing projects of colonialization and discrimination and to invite transformation of this complicity. In this way, formulating and using a land acknowledgment in whatever space one inhabits—educational, recreational, business, or religious—means one is willing to feel the implications of historical discrimination and to acknowledge that the land where education, recreation, business, and religious practices occur is not legitimately owned by those who currently own those spaces. Returning land to Indigenous peoples is one possible outcome that may come of routine use of these acknowledgments that reveal the ongoing situations of injustice that allow some people to thrive but not others. Wide-scale transformation of our economic models around ownership of land and residences and the cultivation of practices of sharing are implicated in the experience of recognizing that land in fact has been stolen from Indigenous peoples—and that many others have profited and continue to profit from this past theft of land—and providing remediation.

THE THANKSGIVING ADDRESS: GREETINGS TO THE NATURAL WORLD

The Thanksgiving Address emerged from practices associated with the Haudenosaunee peoples of upstate New York and Canada. The Haudenosaunee, or Six Nations peoples, comprise families of Mohawk, Oneida, Cayuga, Onondaga, Seneca, and Tuscarora peoples. When they gather for deliberative or ceremonial purposes, the Thanksgiving Address is voiced as a means of experiencing the people's unity with all that is—this affirmation of unity forms the bedrock on which all subsequent deliberation or ceremony can proceed. Though a person might voice parts of the Thanksgiving Address in ways unique to that person or their family, the comprehensive manner in which all parts of creation are addressed and thanked remains constant. Expressing this address not only allows all present to begin deliberations or celebrations with a common frame of mind but also allows for communal acknowledgment of shared vulnerability and a unified experience of gratitude for all that gives them life. The address begins,

> Today we have gathered and we see that the cycles of life continue. We have been given the duty to live in balance and harmony with each other and all living things. So now, we bring

our minds together as one as we give greetings and thanks to each other as people. Now our minds are one.

We are all thankful to our Mother, the Earth, for she gives us all that we need for life. She supports our feet as we walk about upon her. It gives us joy that she continues to care for us as she has from the beginning of time. To our mother, we send greetings and thanks. Now our minds are one.[2]

The address goes on to acknowledge such various aspects of creation as waters, fish, plants, food plants, medicinal herbs, animals, trees, birds, winds, Grandfathers / Thunder Beings, Brother Sun, Grandmother Moon, the stars, enlightened teachers, and the Creator / Great Spirit.

The familial language that begins with Mother Earth, affirming the sustaining source of our human life, and continues with the address of various parts of the Earth community as siblings and grandparents resonates with St. Francis of Assisi's Canticle of Creation. Noting this resonance helps us see that there is not the kind of dissonance between Christian and non-Christian life that Christian settlers of the Americas wanted to temper by imposing their own traditions on Indigenous peoples whom they considered pagan. Rather, the resonance reveals the deep levels of continuity between traditions that emphasize creature and creator relationships, allowing those who inhabit the "creature" category to recognize their joint status as making them kin.

The Thanksgiving Address invites us to a deep recognition of familial relationship across creation as the expression of giftedness. All these creature-kin exist as gifts to one another and, by implication, the human speaker and the human community engaged in this ecospiritual practice of the Thanksgiving Address might too discover their deep giftedness for all creation. For too long, human presence, especially when those most powerful among the human community sought to eradicate voices that would promote healthy and flourishing Earth-human relations, has had a negative impact on the natural world. We are invited to consider how we might repair the damage we have done by living into a new understanding of ourselves as recipients of nature's gifts and as able to offer our own gifts back to nature.

Though many of us in the United States have grown familiar with Thanksgiving as a family holiday celebrated in the fall season, today, many places of education and religious worship are transforming their experience of this festive time commemorating gratitude with enhanced historical understanding of the colonizers' reliance on and exploitation of Indigenous communities for integration into this new land centuries ago. What would have happened if these ancestors of many Americans today had been more respectful of Indigenous practices and worldviews, and adopted a way of living with the communities already existing in mutually beneficial ways in the land these colonizers saw as so plentiful and giving? What would our world today be like if we had centuries ago adopted thanksgiving as a routine dimension of every gathering? The Thanksgiving Address offers us language to give voice to the elements of our world that daily give us life and pleasure.

THE HONORABLE HARVEST

Use of the natural world is a normal part of our relationship with the natural world. When use is exploitation, we distort that relationship of kinship in favor of our exercising our (limited) powers over others: animals, plants, the land in general. Robin Wall Kimmerer's work engages the necessary interactions with the natural world that may trouble purists. For instance, her own misgivings about hunting are voiced with transparency as she gets to know a trapper whose care for the populations of animals he traps extends to monitoring litters and making sure he does not overextend his use of these animals' bodies for food and for their furs. He also is conscientious about helping them get through rough winters by providing food from his own stores. These activities are presented as means by which a human operates as a regulator within an ecosystem, a role mentioned in a Council of All Beings writing in a previous chapter. Conscious and conscientious inquiry into the impact of one's use of the natural world is the basis of the Honorable Harvest.

The Honorable Harvest, as presented by Robin Wall Kimmerer in her book *Braiding Sweetgrass*, includes the rules associated with using the natural world in an honorable way by the Indigenous traditions Kimmerer is familiar with. Though not written down in quite the same way as other hunting and gathering procedures that a hunter or fisher must know before procuring a license, the principles of the Honorable Harvest nevertheless, Kimmerer argues, should be known by all who engage the natural world for what may be taken from it through hunting, fishing, foraging, and similar activities. If the principles were to be written down, Kimmerer suggests a few ways they might be articulated. Her book describes the ways Indigenous peoples demonstrate the following principles:

> Know the ways of the ones who take care of you, so that you may take care of them.
> Introduce yourself. Be accountable as the one who comes asking for life.
> Ask permission before taking. Abide by the answer.
> Never take the first. Never take the last.
> Take only what you need.
> Take only that which is given.
> Never take more than half. Leave some for others.
> Harvest in a way that minimizes harm.
> Use it respectfully. Never waste what you have taken.
> Share.
> Give thanks for what you have been given.
> Give a gift, in reciprocity for what you have taken.
> Sustain the ones who sustain you and the earth will last forever.[3]

I bet many of these principles of the Honorable Harvest may remind you of other activities and perspectives you have observed that are consistent with environmental activism and a more explicit care relationship between humans and their environment. This consistency reminds us of the foundational ethic or set of values that Indigenous wisdom offers all cultures as we navigate a difficult time of climate transition. These rules might govern an individual's behavior, as Kimmerer describes when she goes out into the field to do her work as a scientist and harvests plants she needs as specimens for her research in a way consistent with this ethic. Surprisingly, some of her research shows that sweetgrass, in particular, flourishes when harvested in an honorable way. Being left alone, as some environmental advocates or conservationists might argue, is not the best policy for some, if not many, parts of creation with which humans interact. A reciprocal relationship has grown up over time, changing the actual identities and needs of many parts of creation they coevolve in relationship. This applies to aspects of creation known to us and also to our own coevolving relationship with creation. Though not the typical parameters that would usually determine a scientist's interactions with the natural world, the Honorable Harvest restores dignity and respect to the work of science and the relationship the scientist has with the natural world she studies. These principles can also speak to the rest of us when we consider what and how we harvest, whether we are out in a field or forest ourselves. In what way is our purchase at the supermarket reflective of the principles of the Honorable Harvest? Could, in fact, a restoration of our dignity—our honor—be an essential gesture of our time, needed to restore relationships broken by centuries of exploitative use of the natural world? Such taking care of others implied by the principles of the Honorable Harvest results in what Linda Hogan calls the "solution to the mystery that we are."[4] Abiding by these principles offers us an opportunity to not only express our acknowledgment of and thanksgiving for how the natural world supports us every moment but also resume a kind of indigenous dignity that all of us are capable of. As Kimmerer writes, becoming indigenous is something we all are invited to as we live with fuller consciousness of our impact on the natural world and our relationship with all components of the natural world.

PERSONHOOD AND PERSPECTIVISM: NEW PRONOUNS FOR NATURE

Our use of language emerges from and reinforces assumptions consistent with our worldviews. A main characteristic of animistic thought is that personhood may be understood to characterize diverse forms of life beyond the human. This kind of understanding is consistent with many Indigenous peoples' way of regarding others. Though we might actually feel pretty comfortable talking about a beloved animal companion who has personality, few of us use language routinely to reflect recognition of personhood. And what about when we think of other animals, or even what we consider and refer to inanimate objects as? Does this inanimate quality of their being constitute a lack of personhood? Or might we be able to think, using the lens of Christian creatureliness and relationships between Creator and creature, of all "things" that have been created through the lens of personhood?

Graham Harvey defines animists as "people who recognize that the world is full of persons, only some of whom are human, and that life is always lived in relationship with others."[5] Many Indigenous peoples have no problem regarding and speaking of other life-forms as Snake People, Rock People, and so on.[6] The Lakota sweat lodge ceremony, for instance, involves the participation of heated stones lovingly regarded and referred to, welcomed into the space, as grandmother and grandfather. Does this mean that all other life-forms, all animals, all stones or mountains, rivers or bodies of water are persons? In a way, no. Indigenous cultures draw understanding of personhood from relationship. A being is regarded as a person when that being has a relationship to another, creating an effect for or on the other. One example of this might involve how the sun and moon "govern our activities" (this is even reflected in the language of the Bible's first creation story) when these bodies in the sky rise or set. They effect a response from us, in that we either go to bed and sleep or get up and start our work. In our planetary setting, these celestial bodies are extremely significant and thus, for us, feature as persons. Similarly, if we are walking along a forest path and come to a rock in our way and move to walk around it, the rock has affected us, governed our behavior, which makes it possible to relate to the stone as *person*. The rock has evoked a response from us, and we have entered into a kind of relationship with the rock merely by altering our steps along the path and going around it.

Perspectivism is an outlook that seems to run aside Thomas Berry's maxim that we live in an Earth community that is a communion of subjects and not a collection of objects. This maxim emphasizes the subjectivity of all life-forms and explains that all of us experience the same things, though through different embodied realities. For instance, the sun gives off heat that a tree and a human being will both experience but in different ways, given the different forms or substances of their beings that soak in the sunshine. Perspectivism is the basis for articulating a creaturely continuity between all living beings—we experience the same external circumstances and even mutually influence each other's realities, and we can sense to differing degrees of accuracy, therefore, what another creature experiences. Though I cannot know what a tree experiences while soaking up moisture from its roots through soil, I can consider what my own body feels like when my limbs (note that we use the same word to speak of tree and human parts) are in contact with moisture, and we can draw from our creaturely continuity to empathize with how a tree might feel or what they might experience when not getting enough moisture. Similarly, we may not know what a bird on Midway Islands experiences when eating plastics that are littering its natural food supply, but we do know through our own embodied experience how it feels to eat items, whether food or not, that are not good for us. The similar lack of moisture and the upset to our digestive processes that we experience enable us to enter empathically into the trees' and birds' experiences and even make changes when we recognize that our own actions are the cause for why forests are dry and more vulnerable to devastating fires and why birds are suffering in habitats where their food has been replaced by what is not food. In addition, because we care for our own young, we can empathize with the birds' desire to feed their young, and we can grieve when seeing them feed their offspring plastics.[7]

Robin Wall Kimmerer suggests reinvigorating a grammar of animacy in our language. What she means by this is to let our language reflect our awareness, as humans, that much lives in the world beyond ourselves. If such awareness is incipient or not well-developed, conscious selection of the ways we communicate using language might cultivate this awareness and encourage its growth. Sometimes, the "fake it until you make" strategy is key to developing new capabilities and skills, and in this case, a grammar of animacy would reflect the agency of living beings by focusing on verbs rather than nouns and inflecting those verbs according to animate or inanimate qualities. For instance, Kimmerer describes how "being a Saturday" and "being a bay" are both verbs that can be expressed in her native Anishinaabe language without the nouns Saturday and bay. Being a Saturday and being a bay are activities and reflect the energetic, dynamic, and animate quality of parts of our lives that most of us typically designate with static language of the noun. Further, the activities described by using verbs like this also implicates volition or decision-making on the parts of other aspects of creation, letting us reflect in our language the possibility that other parts of creation, beyond the human, expresses intelligence, even if a different kind than we usually are familiar with. Verbs emerging from a grammar of animacy can indicate a decision on the part of the water contained in space to be a bay.[8]

Moreover, though Kimmerer delights in what scientific investigation makes possible in deepening our understanding of the natural world, she also critiques the objectifying stance adopted by scientists (and often the rest of us) that is expressed with the language of "it." We may look out a window and see a squirrel and wonder what "it" is doing. An immediate remedy for the objectification implied by the word "it" is to supply gendered pronouns such as she or he, or the plural they when we are unsure of gendered identities. Kimmerer, however, suggests the creation of new pronouns to affirm the subjectivity of others with whom we share our planetary home. She draws on part of the word in her native Anishinaabe language that indicates the beings of the living earth in order to suggest that "ki" (singular) be used in place of "it" when we might speak of birds, insects, animals, trees, mountains, forests, and so on. To create a plural for this word, she suggests "kin," which already has rich associations with the way some have regarded beings of the natural world. Kimmerer asks us to do a thought experiment about how we might refer to our own grandmothers: "Imagine your grandmother standing at the stove in her apron and someone says, 'Look, it is making soup. It has gray hair.' We might snicker at such a mistake; at the same time we recoil. In English, we never refer to a person as 'it.' Such a grammatical error would be a profound act of disrespect. 'It' robs a person of selfhood and kinship, reducing a person to a thing."[9] This change in designation might seem small, but as we try it out, we may discover that a different way of being in relationship with others emerges from such small shifts in our language. A similar strategy for effecting such a shift is to speak of "somebody" rather "something" when indicating another life-form. "Somebody has been here," we might remark when looking at tracks on the seashore or in the forest; "Someone is hungry," we might remark as we watch an animal feed ki's young. Rehabilitating the values encoded within Indigenous languages and worldviews is a work of reparation for those of us who are part of cultures responsible for enforcing assimilation of Indigenous peoples through not permitting Indigenous peoples to use their own languages or to practice their own religions. There are far greater reparations that we are invited to in terms of land ownership that may have greater energy coalesce around them as we attend in smaller ways to the gifts of sensibility and sustainability that Indigenous cultures offer. As Kaitlin B. Curtice writes, "If Christianity is able to de-center itself enough to see that the imprint of Sacred Mystery already belongs all over the earth, to all peoples, it would change the way we treat our human *and nonhuman* kin."[10] Curtice writes as a Christian citizen of the Potawatomi Nation, exploring the project of decolonization that other Christians might join.

CONCLUSION

Countries are beginning to establish political frameworks for recognizing the rights of landforms such as mountains, forests, and rivers. This recognition is made possible when a biocentric or geocentric orientation is adopted instead of an anthropocentric perspective. Other parts of our life or Earth community have a right to the kind of circumstances that enable them to survive and even thrive. As we value the insights of animistic thought and perspectivism, we realize that we share more in common with other beings and have a greater desire to participate in and contribute to the well-being of these other aspects of our Earth community.

Of course, when the rights of the natural world come into conflict with rights adhering to other parts of the community, then, of course, adjudication of some kind has to happen, and a larger perspective is adopted so that the fullest version of impacts is analyzed. Similarly, perspectives through time have to be drawn into consideration: Will actions taken today determine the fate of parts of our landscapes or Earth community in the next decade? Will certain actions facilitate survival and flourishing or inhibit such survival and flourishing? As we answer these questions, what actions do these understandings lead us to? Specifically, what responsible actions do they lead to—that is, actions that are *responsive* to our Earth community and the Earth community's various needs?

Indigenous traditions offer all people of goodwill resources for recovering a relationship with the natural world conducive to mutual flourishing. Some of the habits and principles described in this chapter emerge as ecospiritual because they contribute to a person and a community understanding more fully how they belong within the Earth community and that their life-sustaining energies are replenished by their belonging within the Earth community. Acknowledging that the land most of us are on in various colonized countries once belonged to others and should in fact still belong to others expresses implicitly a desire to restore right relationships with those who have had their lands stolen from them. A land acknowledgment requires that we look into the hidden histories of our community's unethical treatment of Indigenous peoples and give name to the families who not only have thrived historically but continue to thrive in areas where we live. A land acknowledgment can invite us to include communal agreements about the way we will not only acknowledge but repair past broken relationships. Similarly, the Thanksgiving Address and Honorable Harvest initiate us into attitudes of shared gratitude with all human beings for the various ways the natural world provides us with the means of continued life. Changing the language we use to refer to these neighboring beings, from objectifying them to familiarizing them to us by acknowledging our family relationships, offers us an everyday way to make more substantial changes in our identity as beings in right relationship with others.

Questions for Reflection and Discussion

- How visible or present are Indigenous peoples, concerns, and values in your community? Are they represented authentically, or have they been commodified? How do you know?
- Have you experienced a setting in which a land acknowledgment was made? How did that feel? Where might you introduce this practice yourself?
- How do practices of thanksgiving appear in your life? Just during the holiday season? Or are there other ways to habitually, even daily, express thanksgiving?
- What aspects of the Honorable Harvest appeal most to you, and why? How might you further implement one of these Honorable Harvest principles in your life?
- If braiding were an image to make sense of the convergences of your life, what strands would it involve? What are the threads or grasses that your life braids?

Suggested Ecospiritual Practices

Meditate with the words of the Thanksgiving Address, the full text of which you can find online. Learn by heart pieces of it that most speak to you, that especially allow you to voice the appreciation you already feel, and that invite you to deeper acknowledgment of every being that facilitates and shares your existence. Consider occasions to bring these words of appreciation and to evoke unity in gatherings of which you are a part and use the opportunity to reflect with friends on the value of gratitude in your lives. Consider this an invitation to grow more attentive to how others express gratitude and to how shared expressions can deepen your own awareness of all you have to be grateful for and for the various unities we share. You might also meditate with music or poems by the esteemed Joy Harjo, a member of the Muscogee Nation. Her poems provide good opportunities to practice *lectio divina* with its movements of reading, reflecting, responding or resolving, and resting. Try "Praise the Rain" and "Eagle Song." Also try "Remember," which is a powerful invocation to all the human and other ancestors with whom we share a life story.[11] Sit with the poem and maybe add some lines that describe the particular aspects of your own life you need to be called to remember. Let this poem work as an invocation to call you to your own indigenous dignity—a person called to live in ways that reflect conscious care for future generations. Consider this an invitation to remember your true identity as a member of a family just like others.

Become conscious of how you use language to speak of other creatures. Can you find ways to avoid objectification in your mindset and language with use of "ki" or "kin" rather than "it" to speak of animals and plants? How does it feel when you do this? When speaking with others, how do they respond to this adaptation in your language, meant to contribute to the work of solving the mystery that we are? Consider this an invitation to experiment with the power of language and your own ability to change and adapt, fostering new relationships of interbeing.

For Further Reading

Braiding Sweetgrass: Indigenous Wisdom, Scientific Knowledge, and the Teachings of Plants by Robin Wall Kimmerer (Milkweed, 2013)

Dwellings: A Spiritual History of the Living World by Linda Hogan (W. W. Norton, 1995)

Native: Identity, Belonging, and Rediscovering God by Kaitlin B. Curtice (Brazos, 2020)

Sacred Instructions: Indigenous Wisdom for Living Spirit-Based Change by Sherri Mitchell (North Atlantic, 2018)

Shalom and the Community of Creation: An Indigenous Vision by Randy S. Woodley (Eerdmans, 2012)

CHAPTER EIGHT

Implications for the Twenty-First Century

When we love the earth, we are able to love ourselves
more fully.

—bell hooks, *Sisters of the Yam:*
Black Women and Self-Recovery

We are only about a quarter into the new millennium, and dire pre-
dictions about the future we are creating are disturbing more and
more people. Various reports offer us differing benchmarks for slow-
ing down global warming by curtailing carbon emissions that must
be reached by certain decades in order for human life to be sustained
on planet Earth. Whether or not we can as a species meet these
benchmarks is still unknown, and youth climate activists are calling all of us to give greater attention to the gravity of this situation
and the implications for the future that we leave for them and their
children. The values of faith, hope, and love might inform our consideration of these implications. These values are named together by
the apostle Paul in his letter to the Corinthians and its passage that
famously celebrates love: "Love is patient; love is kind; love is not
envious or boastful or arrogant or rude. It does not insist on its own
way; it is not irritable or resentful; it does not rejoice in wrongdoing,
but rejoices in the truth. It bears all things, believes all things, hopes
all things, endures all things. Love never ends . . . And now faith,
hope, and love abide, these three; and the greatest of these is love"

(1 Cor 13:4–8, 13). While we might take issue with some of the ways Paul characterizes love and say that what is often called "tough love" might mean not bearing all things, for instance, when they contribute to oppression or abuse, this ancient passage from a sacred text does draw together some useful ideas about what it might mean to be a lover at this stage in our human history. Love might require us to listen deeply to one another, especially those most vulnerable to the effects of climate change. It might require us to do the difficult work of facing the truth about our own complicity in causing climate change. It might require us to temper our enthusiasm as consumers eager to keep up with the latest gadgets and electronic devices, envious of the wealthy who readily afford them.

What about faith and hope? Just as love might assume a greener hue as we think about how it might reframe our actions and attitudes toward others accompanying us through a time of substantial environmental and cultural change, so too might faith and hope be greened. A green faith might emphasize the aspect of a person's approach to life that is confident and empowered to make a difference, however small, in the outcome of our current climate catastrophes. A green faith might enable a person to live into the fullness of their ability to live with integrity that matches their inward values with outward action and to live with courage to make difficult decisions about their future and their activities that promote or prevent the flourishing of the Earth community. Green hope, similarly, might enable us to live resolutely from the optimism that is so hard to come by these days as changes that are out of our control threaten our work, our families, our homes, and the ways we will obtain food and things necessary for our survival in upcoming decades. Green hope enables us to resist giving in to paralyzing fear or to what has come to be known as ecoanxiety or ecodespair—feelings of anxiety or despair arising as a response to ecological crises. A green faith, green hope, and green love spring from the seeds of our lives as spiritual beings living in communion with Earth community members and enabling us to live more equitably and in a way that directly promotes our health and well-being in ways that capitalism, consumerism, and addiction do not.

As our human consciousness about our earth home began to expand when the astronauts on Apollo 8 looked back at "earthrise" on their space tour around the moon, we have an enlarged sense of the appropriateness of attaching "eco" as a prefix for so many new dimensions of our lives opening up. We might add this prefix to our disciplinary engagements with knowledge and behavior that are colored by this new consciousness. As Thomas Berry wrote,

> From here on, for an indefinite period, the main difference between human beings will not be the difference of conservative or liberal, based on political, social, or cultural orientation, as has been the case for humans in the Western world throughout the twentieth century. Rather, it will be the difference between . . . those who exploit the planet in a deleterious manner and those who sustain the planet in its integral functioning. This difference will provide not only the public identity of individuals; it will also be a primary designation in the professions: law, medicine, education, religion, or politics. The prefix "eco-" will occur in a multitude of words that will refer to the coherence of ideas, actions, or institutions in relation to the integral life systems of the planet.[1]

Berry's insight refers to a time, right now, when deliberate attention needs to be focused on greening these various aspects of our common life. We might hope, though, that in the future such a prefix becomes irrelevant because everything and everyone will be oriented toward sustaining the planet in its integral functioning.

FAITH

Faith is a fundamental dimension of most spiritual traditions. Faith means radical trust and is often distinguished from belief, which it may nevertheless resemble. As a person's experiences evolve over time, their beliefs may change, and their ability to hold open questions without answers, to tolerate uncertainty, and even to celebrate mysteries and the unknown may grow. These transformations in one's abilities constitute faith. Faith in what, though? In whom? For some traditions, faith in God is the most important dimension of faith. Faith in others, faith in a community, faith in oneself may all become components of understanding how a relationship with God unfolds. In the context of twenty-first-century crises, faith is an uncertain commodity. Many institutions and the behavior of their figureheads have caused people to *lose* faith in them. This is true in the arena of politics, religion, education, the corporate world, Hollywood, and even science. A crumbling of confidence as to where we might legitimately direct our faith seems to describe the experience of many today.

Many religious traditions also warn, however, of idolatry as a perversion of faith. Idolatry indicates the worship of something that likely is not worthy of one's worship. In fact, idolatry refers to an activity that permits something to occupy the place of what might legitimately call forth our love, respect, and reverence. An idol might take physical form, as historically, it might have been a statue of a god, but an idol also might describe anything we allow to have undue influence in our lives as we offer it our deepest and most sacred emotions of veneration. Some of our climate catastrophes today arise from generations of idolizing machines, science, money, and other things that have allowed human progress to unfold in the way it has. Even today, we commonly hear and use the word "idol" to refer to celebrities whose status very few of us will attain but that we are somehow taught to desire.

Idolatry as a misdirection of our deepest feelings can be countered when our faith is summoned from the whole of us—our mind, emotions, body, spirit—and enables us to coexist in harmony with others. What does it mean then to be a person of faith? Though faith is most often thought to be a function of a person's spiritual capacity rather than an intellectual capacity (where beliefs may be entertained and accepted or rejected), faith is also an embodied experience—something that derives its being and its power or functioning from the fact that a person lives. For instance, David Abram affirms the value of an embodied faith, or what he calls a "corporeal faith" when he writes,

> Our greatest hope for the future rests not in the triumph of any single set of beliefs, but in the acknowledgement of a felt mystery that underlies all our doctrines. It rests in the remembering of that *corporeal faith* that flows underneath all mere beliefs: the human body's implicit faith in the steady sustenance of air and the renewal of light every dawn, its faith in the mountains and rivers and the enduring support of the ground, in the silent germination of seeds and the cyclical return of the salmon.
>
> There are no priests needed in such a faith, no intermediaries or experts necessary to effect our contact with the sacred, since—carnally immersed as we are in the thick of this breathing planet—we each have our own intimate access to the big mystery.[2]

In Abram's sense, then, we all are people of faith because we are all people who rely for our ongoing sustenance on air, light, ground, food, and water. Without our ever really considering the full implications of this reliance, we dwell daily in bodies that wake to the assumption that the sun will be present during our day, that we will have air to breathe, that the ground under our feet will not collapse but will hold us upright. Further, we go through our day as people of faith when we find we can communicate and commune with others, human or animal, with language or in silence. We are people of faith when we can trust our senses to give us information about the world around us and our minds to continue to refine that information when we yield to emotional upheaval at the sights, smells, and sounds of the world around us. These are ways in which faith is a concept that characterizes our everyday living. For many religious people, such everyday faith is only changed or given a new framework when God or a sense of the sacred is added to a person's understanding of their experience.

Julia Fehrenbacher's "The Cure for All of It" expresses instructions for how to live into the fullness of an embodied faith.[3] I encourage you to use the poem for *lectio divina*, looking for which of the instructions in the poem strikes you as most difficult or most desired. Where do you need to slow down? Where might you take your shoes off and let your feet connect you with the living earth? Where might you breathe most deeply into the truth of your being sustained every moment by air, as a generous gift of the cosmos? Further, how might practicing a response to this accessible though demanding invitation change you?

Both Abram and Fehrenbacher indicate that faith in what is given us is the foundation to experience trust and to deepen our commitment to live from what is real rather than to evade the real through illusion—which can be tempting when reality, especially that of our century of climate change and ecological crisis, is difficult to face. Fehrenbacher's words, with their urging us to remain present, breathe, pay attention, and be grateful and celebratory toward all that is, remind me that it could be the absence of these behaviors that has crucially contributed to the crises we experience now.

HOPE

Hope is another virtue that acquires even greater force in our contemporary era than it may have had for peoples in the past whose planetary existence was not threatened in the way we know it is today. Joanna Macy and Chris Johnstone, for instance, write of the "active hope" required of people today to meet the challenges of our ecologically compromised landscapes and communities. This active hope is not senselessly optimistic, blithely expecting that good things will come despite our inaction, a sentiment that the English mystic Julian of Norwich voiced when she reported her conviction that because God created, holds, and loves the Earth that "all will be well and all will be well and every kind of thing shall be well."[4] Affirming such hope is a beautiful capacity and yet could render people passive to the work that needs to be done to meet the challenges of our time. Active hope enables us to acknowledge the difficulties involved in maintaining optimism. Active hope consists of courage to be present and respond to what is real.

Ecoanxiety and ecodespair are realities of our time: we are living when anxiety and despair caused by economic and social upheaval are exacerbated by the scenarios forecast by those monitoring climate change. There does not seem to be reason for much hope for the future, and reacting to this with resignation is a severe temptation for many. Others might welcome the catastrophes accompanying climate change in the hope they might precipitate rapid and largescale change. But resignation and bewilderment might be more common and involve hostility and resentment toward others who remain oblivious or indifferent to the challenges continually emergent in our time. In the film *First Reformed*, Ethan Hawke plays a Christian minister who comes to understand the gravity of climate change through the concerns of a member of his congregation. How his character responds to this reality is distressing and not meant to operate as a lesson for any viewer. Rather, the film sympathetically and seriously engages the ecoanxiety and ecodespair that even a person of religious faith might experience when their hope has been radically undermined by seeing how others, who also identify as Christian, value profit over appropriate ecological reform. The minister's clash with a "greenwashing" corporation ushers him into a pretty extreme set of actions that seem to feel consistent with how seriously the minister begins to take news of climate change.

Though the film could overwhelm some viewers today, especially in light of escalating concerns for the environment, the film also sensitively and compassionately documents a Christian's awakening to the climate crisis and his willingness, in fact, to act sacrificially on behalf of Earth. So much in Christian doctrine sets up a particular attitude of exalting sacrifice, even martyrdom. Juxtaposed with this is the minister's relationship with another parishioner and her unborn child and themes of the feminine and of natality—or new life emerging with birth—which grow stronger as the film progresses to a dramatic finish. Rebirth and even resurrection themes emerge as possibilities for renewal despite the threatening scenario so often focused on in the film. The film ends on a hopeful note, expressing conviction that the unknown future (symbolized by the unborn baby) is still present and that when we act compassionately or mercifully—even against our seemingly better interests—to provide the means for new birth to happen and not to take vengeance on those responsible for things we might understand as evil, something beyond our control and ability to fathom may be possible. As Arundhati Roy affirms, "Another world is not only possible, she is on her way. On a quiet day, I can hear her breathing. She is on her way."[5] Musicians Fran McKendree and Ana Hernández sing this affirmation with Julian's words quoted earlier in this chapter in a song called "All Shall Be Well / Another World." Check out their music online and reflect on what promotes your own active hope. What gives you intimations that a new world is being born? The arts are a powerful catalyst for hope, representing an artist's, musician's, or filmmaker's gift of imagination to engage our own use of imagination—gifts that will be needed as we think and act creatively in response to our century of change.

Young contemporary artists such as Billie Eilish and S. G. Goodman integrate music and visual storytelling to reflect on their own identities and transformations. Because of their youth and the dangerous risks that lie before us in terms of climate catastrophe, these young artists share struggles with maintaining hope. Billie Eilish's "My Future" places her in the midst of a dark, rainy landscape where she and the natural world seem permeable. As her musical reflection progresses and she espouses a love for her future, the landscape becomes lit by daylight, and she is supported by growing vines. They seem to embrace her as well in a sort of loving confidence to enable her to remain planted in this optimism for the future. Similarly, S. G. Goodman's "If It Ain't Me Babe" contains visual imagery drawn from her Kentucky home. Goodman's immersive experience of her ecological niche is portrayed in the music video as her avatar is literally grown over with leaves. Both young women seem to be able to identify with the natural world and to allow their beings to be permeated by nature in a fully immersive way, indicating their understanding of a fundamental relationship with the natural world that allows them hope for a future that has room for life that is inclusive of the human. While it is telling that both of these young people identify as women, there is caution to be exercised here in that women perhaps more than men have historically felt themselves to be given over for the other in service when caring for male partners and children. These young musicians' attitudes toward the natural world may seem to convey a willingness to be absorbed by the other in ways that our female ancestors were absorbed by their responsibilities and obligations to others, not often chosen themselves. Nevertheless, the kind of interbeing or fundamental awareness of interconnectedness that these women's songs and videos convey does significantly draw from their femininity as women because of their ability to house life within themselves. Interbeing is a characteristic of female life, and yet while this biological reality is worth consideration, it should not be pushed too far to exclude men from profound experience and exploration of interbeing. All of us, as human beings, may be characterized as communities of creatures—microbially in nature and essential. The English mystic Evelyn Underhill expressed this well:

> We are bound, if we live at all, to accept the fact of a living world outside ourselves, to have social relations with something; and it only remains to decide what these relations shall be. The *yogi* or the hermit who retreats to the forest in order to concentrate [their] mind more utterly upon the quest of God, only exchanges the society of human beings for the society of other living beings. If [they] eliminated all else, the parasites of [their] own body, the bacterial populations of [their] own alimentary system, would be there to remind [them] that [one] cannot live alone. [They] may shift [their] position in the web of life, but [the web of life's] strands will enmesh [them] still.[6]

LOVE

As mentioned in chapter 2, one contemporary movement focused on love is the Order of the Sacred Earth, an intergenerational community that pledges to defend and love Earth to the best of the community members' ability. Many spiritual traditions emphasize practices of loving devotion to God and of compassion toward others and oneself. Greening this compassion means, of course, including the whole of the Earth community—one's immediate neighbors of animal kin and other life-forms within one's bioregion—and the whole of the cosmos, understanding that it may be more reasonable and significant for us to understand our earth and universe homes as *loving us* in creating a place where we humans might emerge as living beings and thrive. Thomas Berry writes of the specificity of expansion in the first moments of the universe (the "big bang" or "flaring forth" or even "primeval orgasm" as ecosexuals call it) that enabled neither explosion nor implosion but just the right relationship of creative tension between exteriority and interiority to effect the coming into being of all that is. Berry speaks of this as an embrace of the universe or the "compassionate curvature" by which all moved into being. Fundamentally rethinking our relationship to our home—our ecological setting—as loving us into being facilitates our own loving return. Love is a fundamental attitude and even choice deriving from and informing our experience of being embodied beings, earthlings. Ecofeminism, ecowomanism, pleasure activism, and ecosexuality are all areas in which to explore the significance of love as a name for the relationship we have with the sacred, our universe, each other, and ourselves.

Ecofeminism describes an approach to ecology, environmentalism, and spirituality facilitated by a deep understanding that the degradation of women and Earth occurs because of a reasoning that women and Earth's life-giving and life-sustaining capacities are to be feared and must be controlled. In some ways, I regard Job, a character in the Hebrew Scriptures, as an early and surprising biblical ecofeminist when he asserted, "Naked I came from my mother's womb, and naked shall I return there" (Job 1:21). What does this little piece of wisdom mean but that Job understands a common fecundity between his mother's body and that of the Earth? Unfortunately, this common fecundity leads to common forms of oppression and exploitation of Earth and women. This, in turn, leads to many women's felt sense of solidarity with the plight of Earth creatures. Notably, there are more women than men involved in feminist and animal rights causes, which identify the harm done particularly to female animal bodies whose reproductive cycles are manipulated for profit as an intolerable situation for a feminist promoting human women's rights. Many of the men involved in these animal rights causes, such as Pete Singer and Tom Regan, are philosophically and ethically engaged without seeming to feel or affirm the personal affective connection with animals that women theorists like Carol Adams and Lisa Kemmerer feel. These men sometimes consider emotions a liability when trying to use reason to affirm animal rights, while female writers like Carol Adams consider the emotions a powerful place to engage a person to change their mind about whether or not animals should be eaten, factory farmed for what their bodies create, worn, or experimented on. Indeed, Adams' radical vegan ethic affirms the connection between the degradation of female human bodies and female animal bodies, like cows and chickens, for the parts of life they create for the giving of life to their own young that humans take from them—milk and eggs. In this way, Adams believes every feminist of whatever gender identity should be a vegan if they truly support the liberation from oppression of female bodies.

Ecowomanism extends this profound approach to discerning hostilities and exploitation of women and Earth to recognize that not all women have been exploited in the same way and to the same degree. On the contrary, women of color have experienced historical and contemporary forms of abuse that give their perspectives on environmental degradation immense value. For instance, scholars such as Melanie Harris and Kimberly Ruffin explore how the experience of women of color in the United States was *as Earth*—that is, they were treated, like Earth, as land and property to be used however an "owner" decreed.[7]

Slave owners treated Black women's bodies as if they might be "harvested" for crops of new slaves just as they harvested their fields for crops of cotton or bred animals to expand their possession of livestock. These similarities are unavoidable in terms of the treatment of women, and ecowomanism attends closely to calling out and repairing these relationships. Despite women's experience of solidarity with creation in its degraded state and of their own degraded situations, it is remarkable that *love* remains a fundamental expression in womanist and ecowomanist experience rather than hate, which might be a more understandable response. As ecowomanist Melanie Harris puts it, drawing on Alice Walker's original formulation of this identification and activity of women of color, "a womanist *loves the Spirit*."[8] Love of all creation is part of the project of effecting personal and communal well-being and flourishing. Similarly, bell hooks affirms the reciprocity of love in our human attitudes as she writes, "When we love the earth, we are able to love ourselves more fully."[9]

Just as feminism is defined as advocacy for women's rights based on an understanding that all people should be treated equally, Harris describes the significance of womanism as a refinement of advocacy that involves empowerment through self-love and love of the earth. She writes, "Perhaps the most well-known part of the *womanist* definition is found at the end of part three, *loves herself regardless*. It is often highlighted as the central point in the *womanist* definition because it captures the spirit of womanism and its primary goals to empower and liberate women of African descent in their communities and the environment in which they live."[10] Reconfiguring identity and creaturely continuity between human and other forms of life on Earth, we can see how the practice of self-love facilitates and extends to love of the natural other and vice versa. Certainly, there are too many times when environmental activists have found themselves burnt out for lack of having performed some kind of self-care alongside their activism. It can feel irrelevant to do so. Similarly, when typical spiritual traditions invite a person to attend to practices that contribute to their own well-being and flourishing, the importance of service or ministry to the world can be neglected. Healing the divide between these two outlooks has been the work of recent sacred activists who see their work of growing social and environmental justice as a form of spiritual practice and a way to avoid burnout by living a balance between work that cares for themselves and cares for others. This balance is not always attainable and yet seems to be the firmest foundation for the work of love for the world and ourselves as a part of the world as we grow a new future together.

Indeed, adrienne maree brown writes of what she calls "pleasure activism,"[11] which rehabilitates focus on what is joyful about working on behalf of others and that counters the typical self-righteousness, judgmentalism, or what some call rigid radicalism[12] that can accompany so many movements for social and spiritual change. Though not all will pursue pleasure in the forms brown writes of, her affirmation of one's right to experience well-being and, even more so, pleasure is a salve to the wounds inflicted by many earnest people committed to revolutionary change, especially in regard to the climate crisis we all face. brown's "pleasure activism" is meant not to induce complacency or escapism but to affirm one's experiential encounter with all that makes life worth living and that reminds us why we care about the environment and why we are willing to do what needs to be done. Pleasure can restore, pleasure can be evocative of all that makes us human, and pleasure can enhance community connections as we learn how to support others' pleasure and to find our own pleasure vulnerable to others' abilities to be with us.

Love relationships are perhaps the most effective in promoting change because all of us want to be loved and to love. Though trauma and dysfunction in relationships may inhibit our ability to feel or express love, at heart our sociability emerges as yearning for the very real communion we provide one another. For this reason, creativity with love relationships is inspiring environmental activists as they promote love as a more effective motivator than fear or shaming. One particular way love relationships are used by activists to call attention to deforestation, for instance, is to ordain or marry trees. Within the ordination context, originating in Buddhist Thailand, trees are ordained priests with a cloth typically worn by human priests in the tradition. This ordination occurs to evoke consciousness of the tree's sacred being and to prevent logging. More relevant to this section on love, the ecoaction of marrying a tree involves a person marrying a particular tree to enable a significant relationship and commitment to form, in which the activist will love and defend their espoused tree. Though a bit strange to our sensibilities and performed mostly in the context of protests or demonstrations, such strangeness is exactly the point and draws attention to the severe precariousness of the situation many trees are in as overlogging damages the health of forest ecosystems. This kind of response has its origins in "tree-hugging," which is, of course, an active embrace of a tree that indicates one's desire to defend and to put one's life on the line between an endangered tree and those prepared to cut the tree down. Often thought to be a derogatory term meant to belittle the affection an environmental activist might feel for trees, in fact this term *tree-hugger* indicates a felt relationship worth preserving and celebrating as more and more trees, and other members of the Earth community, are endangered.

GOING FORTH

Human beings are like a forest, in which some trees are tall and others are short, although all serve their purpose in the ecosystem and all can flourish in different ways.[13]

Wangari Maathai, the Nobel Prize–winning founder of the Green Belt Movement (GBM), ended her book *Replenishing the Earth* with a story of hope and healing. In this story, imagining the creaturely continuity that we humans share with other Earth community kin, Maathai describes a hummingbird trying to put out a forest fire.[14] The hummingbird can only hold a few drops of water in ki's beak, a pittance against the raging flames threatening the forest. Other animals of the forest look on while struggling to protect themselves, and they are scornful of the bird's activity. Yet the hummingbird persists. Maathai explains that the hummingbird's actions are important, even if ineffective alone. She believes that such courageous persistence could be a model inviting collective action, which *does* make a difference. And she believes in the transformative power of acting from one's love for the environment, one's gratitude and respect for Earth's resources, one's self-empowerment and self-betterment, and the spirit of service and volunteerism—all core GBM values—in ways that contribute to the nourishing of our own lives, physical and spiritual, and the nourishing of our communities' lives.

Though some of the greening of individual spiritual practices drawn from varying religious traditions may seem insignificant within the context of a worsening climate crisis, they are nevertheless more significant as they foster community change on a small scale and eventually on a larger scale. Actively working upon the basis of hope, we cannot know whether our actions will catalyze the change that needs to happen in response to our current broken systems—we live in unprecedented times—and yet we do know that these actions can change ourselves, and that is a good place to begin!

Attending to this uncertainty, Joanna Macy wrote that we "cannot know whether we are deathbed attendants to life on Earth or midwives to a new age. Both callings have similar characteristics: a sense of awe, complete attention to each moment, a thinning of the veil between life and death. Whichever side of the coin we are enacting, we are blessed to be of service."[15] "Service" may strike some readers as a demeaning designation of the activity we engage on behalf of others. Though it has specific resonance in religious traditions—indicating in the Christian tradition, for instance, an ideal of how Jesus modeled compassionate ministry to those who needed healing or even just clean feet (John 13:1–17)—the word can sometimes aggravate feminists who object to centuries-long service on behalf of men in authority or service to children in patriarchal societies where gender is constructed along lines that keep women in private spaces, more cognizant of and responsive to the needs of others than to their own needs.

Such ideals of service keep women and other oppressed groups in subjection to those in power and those who can give orders to benefit from their service. Nevertheless, both Macy and Maathai recognize, as women, that they and we need to utilize this value in ways that recognize our own complicity in the degradation of the natural world and our own capacity to foster healing and contribute to renewal. This work has potential to empower us in new ways and to give our lives deeper meaning and purpose, even as we recognize our own needs as being fundamentally met while we work on the behalf of others. In fact, a distinction between oneself and the other seems to dissolve in Maathai and Macy's focus on service. Macy, for example, can speak of the "greening of the self" as the realization of one's larger being as a member and cocreator of all that is, even while it contributes to one's own being and continuance.[16]

In this final chapter, I would like to return to the metaphor of nourishment that also connects one's own flourishing—because of the sustenance we each experience because of the natural world we are a part of—and the flourishing of the larger whole, to which we contribute nourishment in meaningful ways. Though it may feel like our nourishment is just pitifully small drops of water, like those the hummingbird carried to the forest fire, these acts do contribute to our realizing both our self-empowerment and self-betterment. Though this may seem to be a backhanded way to still valorize people's self-sacrificial acts in service to others that can be problematic when assigned to and adopted by marginalized populations, I mean for this valorization of service to come from a changed perspective regarding the identity of self and other. Sensing the continuity between human and other-than-human life in the Earth community and living from this sensibility means we promote our own welfare even as we work on behalf of others. There is no distinction.

The metaphor of nourishment involving seeds, watering, blossoming, and harvest that draws human life into continuity with other life-forms draws a little from a key image representing Joanna Macy's "work that reconnects." Though the phrase "going forth" might contribute too much to the sense of a journey undertaken—a metaphor I earlier critiqued in this book—in Macy's use of the image, it refers to the going forth of new seeds from the maturing plant. The plant image serves as an illustration in some of Macy's books so that we can see the whole cyclic process of *having gratitude* (the plant's roots), of *honoring our pain* (the stems of growth), of *seeing with new eyes* (the flowering plant's blossoms), and finally, of *going forth*, represented by the seeds dispersing to facilitate new life originating elsewhere.[17] Indeed, as we consider new seeds falling away from the plant and being carried by the wind to other places where they will settle and begin new growth, we might think of the Spirit and its ancient associations with wind and the breath of life and how the action of carrying away our new seeds is accomplished by a sacred source and sustainer that is indeed *spiritual* in its identity and functioning. As Jesus reminded Nicodemus when speaking of the Spirit's work in his life and of the renewal involved in new birth, "The wind blows where it chooses, and you hear the sound of it, but you do not know where it comes from or where it goes" (John 3:8). The mysterious and open quality of the work done within us responsive to and contributing to the changes that are a part of our experience in the twenty-first century may be troubling if we want things to be controllable and certain. But these mysterious and open qualities of our lives might also be exciting as we let loose our hold on what, in fact, cannot be managed and controlled and open to radical newness in the play of life always beginning, changing, and being renewed.

Moreover, this plant imagery provides a way of looking at the work involved in growing in awareness of the problems we are a part of in our world today and the really important work of addressing our own response to it so that we are empowered to act in meaningful ways rather than remain paralyzed by anxiety that is not integrated into the energies we need to do the "great work" of our time. As we consider nourishment for a sustainable future, it may be helpful to think of ourselves with this plant image to think about how our lives and what we do with them will contribute to the sustaining of the world, just as we do things in more responsible ways that permit a sustainable future to emerge. As Llewellyn Vaughan-Lee and Hilary Hart write, "Life will give us opportunity after opportunity to live from our hearts instead of our fears or desires, and over time we can recognize these patterns and work up the courage—the power of the heart, *cor*—to respond from a place that is real within us, the place where life has dropped a seed of longing, a seed of truth, a seed of itself. When we live from this inner truth, our lives start to bloom."[18] Blooming lives. Lives that grow fruit to share with others. Lives that grow seeds that go forth from ourselves and create new life elsewhere. All of this is open to us as we create the possibilities for being nourished in our time for a sustainable and flourishing future. Our becoming aware of the truth of our lives means growing comfortable with uncertainty and revision, with changes to our identity as we grow in response to every new possibility that opens to us.

Questions for Reflection and Discussion

- Of faith, hope, and love, which comes easiest to you? Which is hardest to maintain? How do you live these virtues?
- How would you register your ecoanxiety? Is it pretty high or pretty low? How do you manage it? What gives you hope?
- Are you able to sing with Billie Eilish, "I'm in love with my future"? Why or why not? What would allow you to sing this?
- Do you identify with the hummingbird in Maathai's story? Do you feel supported or criticized in what you do or want to do? What might you need to feel more supported?
- What changed worldviews or commitments do you find yourself making having read this book? Why are they important to you?

Suggested Ecospiritual Practices

Find other examples of ecopoetry or ways contemporary musicians, artists, and filmmakers are creating art responsive to climate change. Some of this work can be quite dark, and our response to it might be to feel despair or anxiety—but those feelings themselves may be evoked by artists in order to create the conditions for radical change. Consider this an invitation to grow your feelings of compassion as you listen or engage how artists are addressing the problems of ecological and social injustice and how your own feelings of sadness or anger might spark new actions of solidarity with parts of creation you particularly feel a heart for.

John O'Donohue writes,

> I would love to live
> Like a river flows,

Carried by the surprise
Of its own unfolding.[19]

As you consider what you have learned while reading this book and engaging the questions and suggested practices at the end of prior chapters, consider making an inventory of what new knowledge, values, and skills you have acquired. What has become fluent with your life? What has surprised you? What do you want to learn more about, and how will you do that? What next book might you read, or what new action might you commit to or continue to experiment with? What new chapter in your own life is beginning to be written? Take some time to reflect on how you answer these questions. Additionally, form a small group with others who can offer mutual support as you live more fully your values and commitments. Consider this an invitation to live into your own authority as a person with knowledge of ecospirituality, with ecospiritual values, and with skills to live in an ecospiritual manner that will deepen your love and care for Earth.

For Further Reading

Active Hope: How to Face the Mess We're in without Going Crazy by Joanna Macy and Chris Johnstone (New World Library, 2012)

Elegant Simplicity: The Art of Living Well by Satish Kumar (New Society, 2019)

A Greener Faith: Religious Environmentalism and Our Planet's Future by Roger S. Gottlieb (Oxford University Press, 2006)

The More Beautiful World Our Hearts Know Is Possible by Charles Eisenstein (North Atlantic, 2013)

Replenishing the Earth: Spiritual Values for Healing Ourselves and the World by Wangari Maathai (Doubleday, 2010)

Notes

Introduction

The epigraph is from Fritjof Capra's review on the back cover of Warwick Fox's *Toward a Transpersonal Ecology: Developing New Foundations for Environmentalism* (Albany, NY: SUNY Press, 1990). It is alternatively phrased as "ultimately, deep ecological awareness is spiritual awareness" in Fritjof Capra and Pier Luigi Luisi, *The Systems View of Life: A Unifying Vision* (Cambridge: Cambridge University Press, 2014), 13. This is an important insight from a nontheological viewpoint forming the basis for drawing ecology and spirituality together.

1   I use the phrase the "natural world" a lot in this book. It is not meant to contrast an "unnatural world" or to suggest that some of our indoor settings are not natural themselves, because we and plants and animals can be a part of those settings. Rather, it evokes all that is not manufactured by humans and that forms a part of our common heritage as created beings in our Earth and galactic communities.

2   For good introductions to the field of religion and ecology, see Whitney A. Bauman, Richard Bohannon II, and Kevin J. O'Brien, eds., *Grounding Religion: A Field Guide to the Study of Religion and Ecology* (New York: Routledge, 2011) and Mary Evelyn Tucker and John Grim, *Ecology and Religion* (Washington, DC: Island, 2014). For the companion field of ecotheology, see Celia Deane-Drummond, *A Primer in Ecotheology: Theology for a Fragile Earth* (Eugene, OR: Cascade, 2017). For ecomysticism, see Carl Von Essen, *Ecomysticism: The Profound Experience of Nature as Spiritual Guide* (Rochester, VT: Bear, 2010).

3   Llewellyn Vaughan-Lee, *Spiritual Ecology: The Cry of the Earth*, 2nd ed. (Point Reyes, CA: Golden Sufi Center, 2016), 309; italics mine.

4   Terry Tempest Williams, *Erosion: Essays of Undoing* (New York: Picador, 2020), 214.

5   Christian Wiman, *Ambition and Survival: Becoming a Poet* (Port Townsend, WA: Copper Canyon, 2007), 120.

6   Jane Hirshfield, *Given Sugar, Given Salt: Poems* (New York: HarperCollins, 2001), 73.

Chapter One

1 Eric Daryl Meyer, *Inner Animalities: Theology and the End of the Human* (New York: Fordham University Press, 2018).

2 A geologian might be understood as someone who thinks or talks about the earth (*geo*) rather than or in place of God (*theo*). For Berry, these discourses were the same. While he did not deify Earth in his thinking, he understood the Earth community as expressing something very important about God . . . so, for him, speaking of Earth meant speaking of God and referring to himself as a geologian emphasized this vocation and this self-understanding.

3 The United States is not the only country to have this tainted history. Similar strategies of settlers drawing on biblical authority occurred in Australia (see Norman C. Habel, *An Inconvenient Text: Is a Green Reading of the Bible Possible?* [Adelaide: ATF, 2009]) and in Canada (see Steve Heinrichs, ed., *Unsettling the Word: Biblical Experiments in Decolonization* [Maryknoll, NY: Orbis, 2019]).

4 Lynn White Jr., "The Historic Roots of Our Ecologic Crisis," *Science* 155, no. 3767 (March 1967): 1203–7.

5 Descriptions of the green lens (or what scholars call an ecological hermeneutic) contained in this section are drawn from Habel, *Inconvenient Text*. Examples of this ecological hermeneutic in action can be found in a volume edited by Habel and Peter L. Trudinger, *Exploring Ecological Hermeneutics* (Atlanta: Society of Biblical Literature, 2008) and in the volumes of the *Earth Bible Commentary Series* (London: T&T Clark, 2017–2020).

6 This method enlarges the already fruitful scholarship engaging marginalized human characters in the text. For instance, approaching the Bible with suspicion of its patriarchy requires that one identify with female characters and retrieve wisdom that might have emerged if women had told their version of the stories contained in the Bible.

7 Remarkably, this fear is reinforced in a story that soon follows this creation account (Gen 9:2–4): God is seen as describing the consequences of human lack of responsibility and care and as authorizing human consumption of animal lives in a way that contradicts the earliest biblical vision of a vegetarian human society.

8 This language was introduced by Ada María Isasi-Díaz. See her *Mujerista Theology: A Theology for the Twenty-First Century* (Maryknoll, NY: Orbis, 1996).

9 See Melissa Tubbs Loya, "'Therefore the Earth Mourns': The Grievance of Earth in Hosea 4:1–3," in *Exploring Ecological Hermeneutics*, ed. Peter L. Trudinger and Norman C. Habel (Atlanta: Society of Biblical Literature, 2008), 59–60.

10 This paragraph is based on Eric Daryl Meyer's fascinating reading of this story in his *Inner Animalities*, 98–103.

11 Emily Dickinson, *Letters of Emily Dickinson*, ed. Mabel Loomis Todd (Mineola, NY: Dover, 2012), 349.

12 Denise Levertov, "What the Fig Tree Said," in *Collected Poems* (New York: New Directions, 2013), 905–6.

13 Mary Oliver, "The Poet Thinks about the Donkey," in *Thirst* (Boston, MA: Beacon, 2006), 44.

Chapter Two

1 Athanasius, *The Life of Antony and the Letter to Marcellinus*, trans. Robert C. Gregg, Classics of Western Spirituality (New York: Paulist, 1980).

2 Athanasius, 98.

3 Athanasius, 68–69, 92.

4 Norman Russell, trans., *The Lives of the Desert Fathers: The Historia Monachorum in Aegypto*, Cistercian Studies 34 (Kalamazoo, MI: Cistercian, 1980), 68.

5 Russell, 68 (italics mine).

6 Benedicta Ward, trans., *The Sayings of the Desert Fathers: The Alphabetical Collection*, rev. ed., Cistercian Studies 59 (Kalamazoo, MI: Cistercian, 1984), 234 (adapted to use gender-inclusive language).

7 John Muir, *John Muir: Spiritual Writings*, ed. Tim Flinders (Maryknoll, NY: Orbis, 2013), 107.

8 John Wortley, trans. and ed., *More Sayings of the Desert Fathers: An English Translation and Notes* (New York: Cambridge University Press, 2019), 140.

9 John Wortley, trans., *The Book of the Elders: Sayings of the Desert Fathers; The Systematic Collection*, Cistercian Studies 240 (Collegeville, MN: Liturgical, 2012), 15.

10 Wortley, 19.

11 John Wortley, ed., *The Anonymous Sayings of the Desert Fathers: A Select Edition and Complete English Translation* (New York: Cambridge University Press, 2013), 277.

12 Pope Benedict XVI, quoted in Pope Francis, *Laudato si' [Encyclical on Climate Change and Inequality: On Care for Our Common Home]* (Brooklyn, NY: Melville House, 2015), 133.

13 See David Abram, *Becoming Animal: An Earthly Cosmology* (New York: Vintage, 2011); Paul Wapner, *Is Wildness Over?* (Medford, MA: Polity, 2020); Marc Bekoff, *Rewilding Our Hearts: Building Pathways of Compassion and Coexistence* (Novato, CA: New World Library, 2014); and Bill Plotkin, *Soulcraft: Crossing into the Mysteries of Nature and Psyche* (Novato, CA: New World Library, 2003).

14 His story is told in the book by Jon Krakauer, *Into the Wild* (New York: Villard, 1996) and in a film of the same name (Hollywood: Paramount, 2007).

15 Cheryl Strayed, *Wild: From Lost to Found on the Pacific Crest Trail* (New York: Vintage, 2013). A movie adaptation of her story was made in 2014 (Los Angeles: Fox Searchlight Pictures).

16 Abi Andrews, *The Word for Woman Is Wilderness* (Columbus, OH: Two Dollar Radio, 2019).

17 Sarah McFarland Taylor, *Green Sisters: A Spiritual Ecology* (Cambridge, MA: Harvard University Press, 2007), 67–72.

18 Taylor, 101. Taylor cites Maureen Wild, a Sister of Charity, as the author of these words.

19 SerenaGaia Anderlini-D'Onofrio and Lindsay Hagamen, eds., *Ecosexuality: When Nature Inspires the Arts of Love* (Cabo Rojo, Puerto Rico: 3Way Kiss, 2015), 304.

20 Anderlini-D'Onofrio and Hagamen, 13.

21 Anderlini-D'Onofrio and Hagamen, 79.

22 Matthew Fox, Skylar Wilson, and Jennifer Berit Listung, *Order of the Sacred Earth: An Intergenerational Vision of Love and Action* (Rhinebeck, NY: Monkfish, 2018). See also the Order's website, http://www.orderofthesacredearth.org.

23 For these concepts, consult the work of Richard Louv. For biophobia or nature-deficit disorder, see Richard Louv, *Last Child in the Woods: Saving Our Children from Nature-Deficit Disorder* (Chapel Hill, NC: Algonquin, 2008). For species loneliness, see Richard Louv, *Our Wild Calling: How Connecting with Animals Can Transform Our Lives—and Save Theirs* (Chapel Hill, NC: Algonquin, 2019).

24 Wortley, *Book of the Elders*, 22.

Chapter Three

1 White, "Historic Roots," 1206.

2 Ugolino di Monte Santa Maria, *The Little Flowers of St. Francis of Assisi*, ed. W. Heywood (New York: Vintage, 1998), 36–37.

3 Ugolino, 47–50.

4 Francis of Assisi, "The Canticle of the Sun," in *Francis & Clare of Assisi: Selected Writings*, trans. Regis J. Armstrong and Ignatius C. Brady (San Francisco: HarperOne, 2006), 5–6.

5 Francis, *Laudato si'*, 8.

6 Belden Lane, *The Great Conversation: Nature and the Care of the Soul* (New York: Oxford University Press, 2019).

7 Alan Watts, *The Book: On the Taboo against Knowing Who You Are* (New York: Vintage, 1989), 9.

8   Francis, *Laudato si'*, 42.

9   Francis, 133.

10 Hildegard of Bingen, *Scivias*, trans. Columba Hart and Jane Bishop (Mahwah, NJ: Paulist, 1990), 59–60.

11 Hildegard, 98. Gently adapted to use gender-inclusive language. However, it should be kept in mind that much of the domination/exploitation activity of humans has been effected by men, so I adapt with caution considering that "Man" might be the best word to indicate the human in this particular passage.

12 Hildegard of Bingen, *Book of Divine Works*, ed. Matthew Fox (Santa Fe, NM: Bear, 1987), 373.

13 John Dadosky, "The Original Green Campaign: Dr. Hildegard of Bingen's *Viriditas* as Complement to *Laudato Si*," *Toronto Journal of Theology* 34, no. 1 (Spring 2018): 88.

14 Galway Kinnell, "Saint Francis and the Sow," in *A New Selected Poems* (New York: Houghton Mifflin, 2001), 94.

Chapter Four

1   See Thomas Berry and Brian Swimme, *Journey of the Universe* (New Haven, CT: Yale University Press, 2011), for the full elaboration of these stories. In addition, a film of the book has been made, hosted and narrated by Brian Swimme.

2   Biographical details in this paragraph are drawn from Mary Evelyn Tucker, John Grim, and Andrew Angyal, *Thomas Berry: A Biography* (New York: Columbia University Press, 2019).

3   Thomas Berry, *Befriending the Earth: A Theology of Reconciliation between Humans and the Earth* (Mystic, CT: Twenty-Third Publications, 1992), 21.

4   Thomas Berry, *The Great Work: Our Way into the Future* (New York: Bell Tower, 1999), 12.

5   Berry, 13.

6   Berry, 13.

7   Thomas Berry, *The Sacred Universe: Earth, Spirituality, and Religion in the Twenty-First Century* (New York: Columbia University Press, 2009), 86.

8   Berry, 133.

9   Berry, *Befriending the Earth*, 102.

10 Further, Berry writes that the universe is "the primary religious reality, the primary sacred community, the primary revelation of the divine, the primary subject of incarnation, the primary unit of redemption, the primary reference in any discussion of reality or of value." *The Christian Future and the Fate of Earth* (Maryknoll, NY: Orbis, 2009), 25.

11 Alan Watts and Robin Wall Kimmerer, representing Taoist/Buddhist and Indigenous traditions, respectively, both describe this phenomenon that is only strangely expressed in our human language.

12 Berry, *Sacred Universe*, 176.

13 Daphne Hampson, *After Christianity* (Valley Forge, PA: Trinity Press International, 1996), 10.

14 Berry, *Great Work*, 110.

15 Wendell Berry, *The Art of the Commonplace: The Agrarian Essays of Wendell Berry* (Berkeley, CA: Counterpoint, 2002), 5.

16 Berry, 28.

17 Berry, 285.

18 Berry, 291.

19 Berry, 46.

20 Wendell Berry, "The Peace of Wild Things," in *Selected Poems of Wendell Berry* (Berkeley, CA: Counterpoint, 1998), 36.

21 Wendell Berry, *This Day: Sabbath Poems Collected and New 1979–2013* (Berkeley, CA: Counterpoint, 2013), 20.

22 D. H. Lawrence, "A Propos of Lady Chatterley's Lover," in *Phoenix II: Uncollected, Unpublished, and Other Prose Works*, ed. Warren Roberts and Harry T. Moore (New York: Viking, 1968), 510.

Chapter Five

1 Raimon Panikkar, *The Experience of God: Icons of the Mystery*, trans. Joseph Cunneen (Minneapolis: Fortress, 2006), 32.

2 A collection of reflections by people who have received darshan with Amma is found in *My First Darshan: A Collection of Stories from around the World* (Kerala, India: Mata Amritanandamayi Center, 2003).

3 Shephali Patel, "Darshan," in *Spiritual Ecology: The Cry of the Earth*, ed. Llewellyn Vaughan-Lee (Point Reyes, CA: Golden Sufi Center, 2016), 267.

4 Patel, 279.

5 Patel, 279.

6 Ignatian Solidarity Network, "Eco-Examen Summary," *Reconciling God, Creation and Humanity: An Ignatian Examen*, accessed August 29, 2021, https://www.ecologicalexamen.org.

7 Arthur Waskow, "What Is Eco-kosher?," in *This Sacred Earth: Religion, Nature, Environment*, ed. Roger S. Gottlieb, 2nd ed. (New York: Routledge, 2004), 275.

8 Waskow, 273.

9 Steven Chase, *Nature as Spiritual Practice* (Grand Rapids, MI: Eerdmans, 2011), 225–41.

10 Rev. Solveig Nilsen-Goodin and the Wilderness Way Community, *What Is the Way of the Wilderness? An Introduction to the Wilderness Way Community* (Des Moines, IA: Zion, 2016), 30.

Chapter Six

1 adrienne maree brown spells her name with lowercase letters. Her book to which I refer in this section is called *Emergent Strategy: Shaping Change, Changing Worlds* (Chico, CA: AK, 2017). Her more recent book, *Pleasure Activism*, is also worth checking out for the way it resists default thinking about working for change being characterized as a painful struggle.

2 See, for instance, Charles Eisenstein, *The More Beautiful World Our Hearts Know is Possible* (Berkeley, CA: North Atlantic, 2013), 40–41.

3 brown, *Emergent Strategy*, 41–42. Note that some of these, particularly the mention of water, draw specifically from the Taoist spiritual insight mentioned above. I recognize my debt to brown's examples in this list of principles!

4 Berry, *Sacred Universe*, 71.

5 Berry, 72.

6 See Pope Francis, *Laudato si'*, particularly paragraphs 20–22.

7 For a fuller engagement of zero waste as ecospiritual practice see my article "Of Trash and Treasure: Implications of Zero Waste for the Spiritual Life," *Spiritus* 19, no. 1 (Spring 2019): 81–101.

8 Attributed to the eighteenth-century chemist Antoine-Laurent de Lavoisier.

9 Kimberly Ruffin, "Bodies of Evidence: A Forest Therapy Guide Finds Her Church," *Emergence Magazine*, January 22, 2019, https://emergencemagazine .org/essay/bodies-of-evidence/.

10 Kimberly Ruffin, "A Forest Walk," *Emergence Magazine*, March 24, 2019, https:// emergencemagazine.org/podcast/a-forest-walk/.

11 Muir, *John Muir: Spiritual Writings*, 106. Bracketed material mine.

12 Muir to Ezra S. Carr, ca. 1870, in *The Life and Letters of John Muir*, ed. William Frederic Badè (Cambridge, MA: Riverside, 1924), chap. 8, https://vault .sierraclub.org/john_muir_exhibit/life/life_and_letters/chapter_8.aspx.

13 This section describing Joanna Macy's account of a family practice that allowed her to understand the work she and John Seed were beginning with the Council of All Beings is recounted in *A Wild Love for the World: Joanna Macy and the Work of Our Time*, ed. Stephanie Kaza (Boulder, CO: Shambhala, 2020), 152.

14 Joanna Macy, *World as Lover, World as Self* (Berkeley, CA: Parallax, 1991), 203.

15 Macy, 198–205.

16　See, in particular, pages 79–90 and 97–116 in John Seed, Joanna Macy, Pat Fleming, and Arne Naess, *Thinking like a Mountain: Towards a Council of All Beings* (Gabriola Island, BC: New Catalyst, 2007).

17　This section has been slightly edited. It gives voice to a mountain gorilla's experience and was written by Meg Bender-Stephanski, a member of my fall 2019 ecospirituality class and a co-facilitator of the first ever ecojustice immersion offered during spring break of 2020 through the Moreau Center at the University of Portland.

18　This section giving voice to salmon's experience was written by ecospirituality student Madison Thibado.

19　This section was authored by ecospirituality student Macey Schondel.

Chapter Seven

1　Native Governance Center, "Tips for Acknowledging an Indigenous Land Acknowledgment Statement," *A Guide to Indigenous Land Acknowledgment*, accessed August 29, 2021, https://nativegov.org/a-guide-to-indigenous-land-acknowledgment/.

2　"Haudenosaunee Thanksgiving Address: Greetings to the Natural World," trans. John Stokes and Kanawahienton, Six Nations Indian Museum and the Tracking Project, 1993, accessed August 29, 2021, https://americanindian.si.edu/environment/pdf/01_02_Thanksgiving_Address.pdf.

3　Robin Wall Kimmerer, *Braiding Sweetgrass: Indigenous Wisdom, Scientific Knowledge, and the Teachings of Plants* (Minneapolis: Milkweed Editions, 2013), 183.

4　Linda Hogan, *Dwellings: A Spiritual History of the Living World* (New York: W. W. Norton, 1995), 115.

5　Graham Harvey, *Animism: Respecting the Living World* (London: Hurst, 2019), xvii.

6　For a good example of expressing relationships with peoples of all kinds, see Hogan, *Dwellings*.

7　Chris Jordan's photographs have been mentioned already, but his film, *Albatross*, also details the devastation of pollution on bird bodies, habitats, and practices of care among themselves.

8　Kimmerer, *Braiding Sweetgrass*, 54–55.

9　Robin Wall Kimmerer, "Nature Needs a New Pronoun: To Stop the Age of Extinction, Let's Start by Ditching 'It,'" *Yes!*, March 30, 2015, https://www.yesmagazine.org/issue/together-earth/2015/03/30/alternative-grammar-a-new-language-of-kinship.

10　Kaitlin B. Curtice, *Native: Identity, Belonging, and Rediscovering God* (Grand Rapids, MI: Brazos, 2020), 50.

11   Joy Harjo, *How We Became Human: New and Selected Poems* (New York: W. W. Norton, 2002), 42.

Chapter Eight

1   Berry, *Sacred Universe*, 137.

2   Abram, *Becoming Animal*, 278; emphasis mine.

3   Julia Fehrenbacher, "The Cure for All of It," HuffPost, November 25, 2015, https://www.huffpost.com/entry/the-cure-for-all-of-it_b_8649812.

4   Julian of Norwich, *The Showings of Julian of Norwich: A New Translation*, trans. Mirabai Starr (Charlottesville, VA: Hampton Roads, 2013), 67.

5   Arundhati Roy, *War Talk* (Cambridge, MA: South End, 2003), 75.

6   Evelyn Underhill, *The Essentials of Mysticism and Other Essays* (Oxford: Oneworld, 1999), 38–39 (adapted to use gender-inclusive language).

7   Melanie Harris, *Ecowomanism: African American Women and Earth-Honoring Faiths* (Maryknoll, NY: Orbis, 2019), 47.

8   Harris, 26.

9   bell hooks, *Sisters of the Yam: Black Women and Self-Recovery* (New York: Routledge, 2015), 135.

10   Harris, *Ecowomanism*, 94.

11   adrienne maree brown, *Pleasure Activism: The Politics of Feeling Good* (Chico, CA: AK, 2019).

12   See Carla Bergman and Nick Montgomery, *Joyful Militancy: Building Thriving Resistance in Toxic Times* (Chico, CA: AK, 2017).

13   Wangari Maathai, *Replenishing the Earth: Spiritual Values for Healing Ourselves and the World* (New York: Doubleday, 2010), 139.

14   Maathai, 185–87.

15   Joanna Macy and Molly Brown, *Coming Back to Life: The Updated Guide to the Work That Reconnects* (Gabriola Island, BC: New Society, 2014), 87–88.

16   Macy, *World as Lover, World as Self*, 183–92. Also excerpted in *Spiritual Ecology: The Cry of the Earth*, ed. Llewellyn Vaughan-Lee, 2nd ed. (Point Reyes, CA: Golden Sufi Center, 2016), 151–62.

17   See, for instance, Joanna Macy and Chris Johnstone, *Active Hope: How to Face the Mess We're in without Going Crazy* (Novato, CA: New World Library, 2012), 39.

18   Llewellyn Vaughan-Lee and Hilary Hart, *Spiritual Ecology: 10 Practices to Reawaken the Sacred in Everyday Life* (Point Reyes, CA: Golden Sufi Center, 2017), 35.

19   John O'Donohue, *Conamara Blues* (New York: Doubleday, 2000), 30.

Index